The Rebel
Derek Roche – Irish warrior, British champion

D1513673

Nigel McDermid

SPORTSBOOKS

The Rebel

Published by SportsBooks Ltd

Copyright: Nigel McDermid ©
September 2004

SportsBooks Limited
PO Box 422
Cheltenham
GL50 2YN
United Kingdom
Tel: 08700 713 965
Fax: 08700 750 888
e-mail   randall@sportsbooks.ltd.uk
Website   www.sportsbooks.ltd.uk

Front cover photograph by Steve Parkin, back cover by Bruce Rollinson.

Typeset in Palatino LT Std

A CIP catalogue record for this book is available from the British Library.

ISBN 1899807 25 X

Printed by Bookmarque, Croydon, England

Derek Roche is a boxer whose dedication and courage typify his sport.

He is a fighter who has savoured sweet success and suffered the bitter heartbreak of defeat.

Yet when I first approached him about writing this book I got the impression he was a little surprised. He recognised there are many other boxers out there whose own stories have gone largely untold.

But while this book reflects on Derek's own career and life outside the ring, hopefully it serves too as some small tribute to all those others involved in what is widely acknowledged as being the toughest sport of all.

For Tracei

In memory of Martin Woods

Contents

Introduction

DEREK ROCHE and his pal Danny Thornton boarded the train at Leeds City Station. The pair hardly looked like typical business commuters – no suits, no ties and no polished shoes. But both were professionals – professional fighters, that is. While others travelled home from work, they were on their way for a work-out at the gym. They carried kit-bags, not suitcases, and sported smiles rather than the weary expressions worn by fellow passengers. It was the late 1990s – a time when people wondered if train bosses were capable of running a bath let alone a rail network and it was of little surprise that the carriages were full to bursting.

The crush was hardly eased by a wild-eyed, wild-haired and wild-mouthed man who, for whatever reason, had chosen to sit down in the aisle of the carriage.

Other passengers, though, were observing protocol and saying not a word in protest.

And, then, on got Derek and Danny. Danny can relate the tale.

"Come on there, pal," said Derek in his lilting Irish manner, "you're causing an obstruction for everyone."

"Fuck off," was the wild man's response.

Now Derek is not a man who always takes kindly to such banter but there is a time and place for everything and a crowded rail carriage is perhaps not the perfect place for a disagreement.

So Derek simply said: "Don't you be messing with me, now."

More abuse followed.

Derek shook his head, aware of the anxious faces of other commuters as the train pulled out, heading west.

It was not long before a train guard emerged, red-faced with overwork. He squeezed his portly frame through the melee, grunting his way towards the rear of the train before stopping as he stumbled across the wild-looking man, still sitting in the carriageway.

He tried out a smile for size and then a scowl and then simply sucked on his teeth and said: "You can't sit there, sir, you're blocking the way."

"So?"

"So, could you stand up and move, sir?"

The man replied with a colourful negative and the train guard turned away. He sighed and began a rib-bruising route back towards the front of the train, leaving passengers clueless as to his intentions.

Happily, though, the journey between the two Yorkshire cities of Leeds and Bradford is short. As the train pulled into the station, the tall, scruffy troublemaker rose to his feet. He breathed deeply, and turned to Derek.

Stabbing a splenetic finger in Derek's direction he spat: "Lucky, for you this is my stop, Paddy."

Derek smiled. "Lucky for you, it's mine too."

Both men climbed down on to the platform, Derek clutching his kit-bag.

The wild man then span around and, with hands clenched and raised, shouted: "Do you want some? Do you want a piece?"

Derek stared back and shrugged. "OK," he said, adding: "Just hold my bag a minute, will you?"

Derek passed the bag, which the bemused man automatically grasped in both hands. A split-second later Derek's right fist crashed into his face.

"It wasn't a big hit," says Derek, "more of a tap, just to put him on his arse and shut him up."

Stunned, as if unable to understand why it was he was now sitting on the concrete platform, the puzzled troublemaker looked up at Derek and then down at the kit-bag still in his hands and then across at the carriage where all the train passengers were applauding.

Derek turned towards the carriage, gave a little bow to the crowd, turned back and retrieved his bag.

He smiled at the now not-so-wild man and said: "And don't you forget to get your ticket punched neither."

Derek and Danny then left the station.

Chapter One

Musical spoons and a return to the ring

OCTOBER 5 2002 – one of the world's oldest rap stars struggled up the steps to the stage. But there were no F-words, there was no finger pointing and the trousers were just a little too tight in the crotch. This was George Hudd and his amazing musical spoons.

George was entertaining the country's oldest association of ex-boxers and he rapped out his rhythm on the cutlery in a shaman-like trance, strutting the boards with as much vigour as his 70 or so years could muster.

He had an audience of hundreds. Most were former fighters from clubs as far apart as Tyneside and Kent who were in Yorkshire to help the association of Leeds ex-boxers celebrate their 50th anniversary.

And celebrate they did. The bar at the working men's club that Sunday afternoon took a caning it may never forget. Staff wilted, guests collapsed but George's spoons rapped on.

It was the Leeds' association's Golden Jubilee in the same year the Queen celebrated her own. Sadly Her Majesty had not turned out for this Leeds event.

The city's Lord Mayor was happy to be there, though, lending an official stamp of approval to the occasion. His invitation had caused some concern before the event, with members worried that the wheels on the civic limousine parked outside might "disappear" during proceedings.

There had also been the question of how to address the Lord Mayor. The matter was raised at committee level and a quick letter was fired off to the Town Hall where someone in the know replied that addressing him as Lord Mayor would be fine.

So at the celebrations everyone called him Bryan.

"That's my name," smiled the former rail worker.

He then gamely donned a pair of gloves, borrowed from the boxing club across the road, stepped outside and gently cuffed three former champions for the press photographer present.

In the background stand high-rise flats that dominate an area once visited by a BBC war correspondent for a TV documentary entitled *Forgotten Britain*.

But despair was not on the agenda that day.

The boxing line-up for the picture included association president Allan Richardson, Crawford Ashley and Derek Roche.

Allan, a former British featherweight champion, had won his title in 1977, when aged 28. He had destroyed Edinburgh's Vernon Sollas at Leeds Town Hall. From the mining village of Fitzwilliam, Allan was a boxer of both huge courage and stamina – he built up his strength, it is alleged, by skipping in pit boots.

One matter about his career has always puzzled me, though – that being how to spell his name. A picture of him in his heyday shows the name on his boxing shorts, spelt Alan. Yet the picture itself is autographed Allan. Various newspaper cuttings use both versions – as well as Allen.

Asked to clarify the situation Allan, Alan or even Allen breaks into a smile and replies: "It don't matter ol' love, it's just a name."

Crawford Ashley, former British, Commonwealth and European light-heavyweight champion, also causes some confusion with his name – many people still call him Gary, which was what he was called before he joined the professional ranks. On one occasion he was listed twice in published rankings – once as Crawford Ashley and again, in the same list, as Ashley Crawford.

As for Derek Roche, there's no such confusion. Even his nickname is easy enough to remember – "The Rebel" is tattooed boldly across his shoulders in large Gothic lettering.

The picture session over, we all trailed back into the club to rejoin festivities. Up the stairs we filed, past an ageing black and white portrait of ex-world champion Alan Minter and into the throbbing concert hall.

Many other familiar faces from the boxing world began to show up, including welterweight James Hare and flyweight Dale Robinson. The pair had trailed down the Pennines together from Huddersfield where they had both been fighting the previous night in front of home fans.

"Come to see how we do things in the big city," quipped one Leeds Loiner, unscrewing the top from the sherry bottle he had just won in the raffle.

James smiled as he was warmly applauded on his win the previous night, having retained his Commonwealth welterweight title.

Dale, too, had won – his tenth fight and tenth victory since joining the paid ranks.

For James and Dale there were still dreams of more titles yet to come.

But for the ex-boxers those days were over.

They were happy, though, to meet old friends and 'foes' and turn back the clock to yesteryear.

The old pugs were not hard to spot among the grey-haired non-boxing guests. Ex-boxers tend to stand out in a crowd.

There are the obvious battle scars, busted hands and broken noses, that boast of bruising bouts and countless sparring.

But there is a dignity, too, that marks out such men.

Speak to an ageing fighter, stare into his eyes and the years peel away as he recalls the glories and heartbreak of harder days.

Hopes may have died but no-one can take away that experience of the fight ring.

And it is that experience that provides a common bond among fighters – one that bridges the generations. The oldest veteran can empathise with the young novice in a way that makes boxing as much a culture as it is a sport.

One instance that comes to mind is of an old pro in his seventies leaving a bar and passing on advice to a teenage amateur about to embark on his fourth or fifth fight.

Edging forward on old legs, the veteran adopted a fighter's stance, fists up and whispered slowly: "Remember, son, watch your man, see the punch then slip and move."

At that moment the old timer took an unexpected step backwards, forgetting he was at the top of a flight of stairs. Before anyone could catch him, down he went, but miraculously he managed to stay on his feet. At the bottom he looked up, fists still aloft. With a faint twinkle in his eye, he smiled.

"Like I said, slip and move." And with that he left, shuffling off towards adventures new.

Few fighters, it seems, regret having been in the sport, even though the majority will have experienced huge disappointments. Boxing, which demands sacrifices like no other sport, seems to provide a spark that rarely fades even after decades away from the ring.

Dennis Yearby, for example, another Leeds ex-pro at the Golden Jubilee event, talks of his fight years back in the fifties, remembering contests as if they were yesterday.

He says he finally came out of the game with some happy memories, his good looks, and, he adds "all my own teeth, bar two."

To some people on the outside, however, boxing is a culture so alien they see no further than the end of unbent noses and boxing remains a much-misunderstood and, all too often, a much-maligned sport.

An old newspaper colleague of mine, who covered many bouts as a sports writer, makes little secret of the fact he himself was never a great fan of the fight game. But he insists that in more than 50 years as a scribe he rarely met a boxer who was not a gentleman in the truest sense of the word.

With so many gentlemen about there was little chance of war breaking out that day at North Leeds Working Men's Club. But, just in case, there were two top referees on hand to ensure fair play. Mickey Vann, a former chairman of the Leeds association, was there with good friend and fellow ref Dave Parris.

Mickey had been presented with a belt only the previous week to mark being in charge of his 100th world title fight. Quite an honour. He had obviously been pleased with the presentation and, ever the showman, had held the belt aloft for the TV cameras before the contest began.

But the fight hit the headlines for other reasons.

It had been the showdown between the then up-and-coming Ricky Hatton and Stephen Smith in Manchester. Stephen's cornerman was his dad, Darkie.

It soon became apparent that Hatton was too powerful for Smith as he swept in bruising body shots from the start.

Smith survived round one but in round two was caught above the eye by a stray elbow from Hatton and took a count. Incredibly, in front of a packed arena of thousands, Darkie suddenly climbed into the ring, strode across the canvas and gave Mickey a piece of his mind as well a firm shove that knocked the referee a few paces backwards.

For a moment it appeared Mickey might hit back but he managed to restrain himself. The fight, though, was over.

All hell broke loose on Sky TV, with promoter Frank Warren's neck threatening to burst its collar and shower the crowd in purple rage. The pundits soon weighed in, suggesting Darkie be banned, fined, or, at the very least, be slowly dipped in boiling oil.

As for referee Mickey, an ex-fighter himself, he seemed to have laughed it all off soon after – glad, he said, to have kept his self-control. "Of course, a few years ago I'd have whacked him," he added, smiling broadly.

As for Darkie, well there are a lot of people, myself included, who do not deny he was wrong but who still felt sorry for him. Perhaps it is a reminder that fathers might be best advised not to corner for their sons – and there was a time when those rules applied.

In the end Darkie said he was quitting the boxing game, the sport he had been involved with for decades, although he was to be given his licence back nearly two years later after appearing before the Board's Stewards.

Darkie was much respected and his predicament was particularly sad for Denzil Browne, Central Area cruiserweight champion, who was propping up the bar sipping apple juice at the Golden Jubilee celebrations.

"Darkie was my manager," said the big man from Leeds.

And talking of managers – Tommy Miller – the oldest manager in Britain and the man who first signed Crawford Ashley, was at the do, aged 86. For a time I had thought it was him playing the spoons.

The Leeds celebrations continued all afternoon and into the evening. Derek and the other boxers signed autographs and shook hands and chatted with the old boys.

It had not escaped Derek's mind, however, that he might well have been among those now ranked ex-boxers himself had he not won his last fight the previous month.

Boxers' careers are rarely long, and those who carry on past their fight-by-date are most at risk of damage. Of course, in the end, it is all a matter of knowing when to quit, but there are few fixed rules – age, weight, number of contests, type of opponents and injuries are all part of the enigmatic equation.

Fighters, though, by their very nature are too often the last to recognise when it is time to go. It was the great Sugar Ray Robinson who said: "You always say: 'I'll quit when I start to slide' then one morning , you wake up and you've slid.' "

Derek had been told by manager, Tommy Gilmour, that at just 30 years of age, it would be time to hang up the gloves if he failed to "perform" against Darren Bruce.

It was no heartless threat from the Glasgow fight boss but genuine concern for Derek, a man he respected, who had suffered a first-round defeat in his bid to regain the British title only a few months earlier. Tommy spelt it out that he was unwilling to watch Derek descend the rankings, becoming merely a 'body' for up-and-coming younger men.

Tommy's own words were: "No one is going to use Derek as a stepping stone while I'm his manager."

Derek's return to the ring had followed an unsuccessful bid to regain the British welterweight title against Neil Sinclair.

Bruce was a tough enough challenge at any time, certainly nobody's mug. Tall and powerfully built, the southerner was ranked in the country's top 10, with a more-than-decent record behind him.

For Derek, victory was vital if he was to prove he still had it in him to continue his career. He is the bravest of fighters and I had guessed it would break his heart to have to call it a day, yet at the same time I did wonder if there was enough gas left in the tank, or if there were just too many miles on the clock.

I was also disturbed to have seen Bruce featured on a video-tape compilation of some of boxing's best knock-outs. He had dispatched a certain Darren McInulty with a stinging shot in round two of their match in September 1998.

Come fight night against Bruce, the omens looked bad when Derek took a count in round one. It was a quick left-right combination that caught him on the chin as he ducked, expecting a hook. Down he went to the canvas. It was one of those moments when the hearts of fans sink.

But Derek recalled the fight. "I wasn't hurt, I had all my senses," he said with a chuckle. "I'd just relaxed for a second and got caught. That's all."

By round three Derek was back in the fight and hounding his man. "I just went back to my old style and kept coming at him."

Bruce responded with some eye-watering low shots and was twice warned.

"I was a bit sore for a few days after those," admitted Derek.

There was head use, too, by Bruce, accidental or otherwise. But Derek was in no mind to let his man off the hook. "As the rounds went by I started to get on top. I could sense he just needed a break, just wanted a rest, but that's the time to keep laying on the pressure and I kept after him all the time. In the end I just had too much for him."

It was an impressive eight-round points victory for the Irishman and one that proved the doubters wrong.

Redundancy from the ring had just been put back. "And I loved every minute of it," gleamed Derek.

Chapter Two

An Irish Childhood

IT was on July 19, 1972 that Derek Roche made his first weigh-in. He tipped the scales at a shade over seven pounds in the maternity wing of Bedford Royal Infirmary.

Bedford?

Now my geography is not that hot but I know that Bedford is in England and I wondered, being the proud Irishman that he is, whether it was a matter that rankled with Derek.

"No," says Derek. "Not at all. Some people might try to wind me up by saying I can't be a true Irishman if I was born in England, but I take no notice of that. I was just two or three months old when my parents took me home to New Ross and that's where I lived 'til I was 18.

"And anyway being Irish is about being brought up in a certain culture and your background, more than exactly where it is that you're born."

He adds: "There was one advantage of being born in England, you know." Derek's eyes twinkle. "And that's I was able to fight for the British title."

Derek grins, leans over and whispers in his lilting Wexford accent: "The purses are not too bad for those fights either."

We're sitting in a corner of Delaney's Bar in Harehills, Leeds, where Derek helps the owner, Joe Delaney. Joe is also Derek's boxing sponsor.

It is a lunchtime and Derek has no fight looming and so is relaxing and sipping on a pint of Guinness. Joe is at the bar winding up a couple of old regulars, which seemingly is one of his favourite pastimes.

Derek tells how, when he first fought for the British crown, manager Tommy Gilmour had phoned from Glasgow, sounding a little anxious. He had asked: "Derek, you're sure, aren't you, that you were born in Bedford?"

"Sure, I'm sure," replied Derek. "I was there at the time."
Clearly the blood does run green.

For those interested in such matters, Derek's birth date means he came into this world under the star sign Cancer, reckoned by astrologers to be a sign of peaceful, sensitive types – not, perhaps, characteristics always associated with the boxing fraternity. A quick reference to the record books, though, reveals that fighters sharing that same horoscope include Mike Tyson, Ezzard Charles, Jack Dempsey as well as the Spinks brothers. So not bad star partners to have.

Derek was brought up in the small inland port of New Ross in south east Ireland in County Wexford. New Ross is the same town in which both his parents, Pat and Liz, were born.

Throughout their childhoods, Pat and Liz had lived no more than 200 yards apart in the Charlton Hill area, though they had hardly known each other as youngsters, there being a three-year age gap between them. It was not until they were young adults, both working in London, Pat as a foreman on the building sites and Liz in factories, that they met each other by chance and, as they say, their romance blossomed.

It was the sixties and England – well, London at least – was supposedly swinging, and love, according to every other pop song of the time, was more or less compulsory. But in many parts of England there was little love for the Irish and prejudice ran deep among some people. In bleak boarding houses of the day, signs could still be found hanging in windows, proclaiming: "No dogs, no blacks, no Irish."

The Roche's first son Paul was born in London and three years later along came Derek by which time employment had taken the family to Bedford, about 50 miles north of the English capital.

But with two young sons to bring up, Liz was becoming increasingly eager to return home to the old country and the decision was made, with Derek no more than three months old, to go back to New Ross where a new council estate, called the Bosheen, was being built.

As it happens, Pat and Liz still live in the house they moved into back in 1972. Their daughter Denise, six years Derek's junior, lives there too.

The town of New Ross is not a big place. Even today its population is only a little more than 6,000. Include its hinterland and that figure swells to nearer 25,000.

It is an inland port, about 25 kilometres from the open sea, built on a steep hill above the tidal waters of the River Barrow. To the south west, and just over the county border, is the city of Waterford, while to the east, but a little further in distance, lies the city of Wexford itself.

I am not employed by the local tourist board but it is fair to say it is a beautiful part of the world and the place that Derek still regards as home in spite of him and his partner Tracei having had a son and put down roots in Leeds.

"I had happy times in New Ross as a boy," says Derek. "We weren't what you'd call rich and that's for sure, but it was a loving family and that's something that I will always appreciate."

He nods his head. He even looks a little wistful.

"Dad was out of work because he'd been injured when he was building a barn and a girder fell on his back, off the back of a wagon."

He speaks in a matter-of-fact manner.

"There was never a lot of money about but we were always out shooting or fishing, as much for the table as for the sport."

Derek smiles and tells a tale about his father and Uncle Johnny. "My dad and his brother are both great shots. They're both stubborn buggers too," he adds.

"I remember one Christmas we were playing cards and talking about hunting and what with the drinks and that my dad and Johnny start to wind the other up. They like doing that."

Derek grins again. "And then dad says, 'ah Johnny you're so good with that gun of yours you can shoot round corners, I bet.'

"Johnny doesn't like this, of course. So up he gets. Not a word. In a mood he is, and off he goes out of the house.

"You know, after that the pair of them never spoke to each other for a whole year. A whole 12 months it was, would you believe? And Johnny only lives just across the road.

"They even passed each other one day down a country lane when my dad was out walking the dog, Tango. Johnny said, 'Hello there, Tango' but he ignored my dad."

Derek shakes his head.

"It wasn't until Christmas day the next year that we got Johnny round again and things were back to normal."

Derek reflects a while longer on his younger years.

"I loved the shooting, the fishing and the ferreting," he continues.

"Not one of the anti-hunting lobby, then?" I wonder aloud.

"And the snaring," adds Derek.

"We were always outside. I guess there wasn't much else for us youngsters at the time in New Ross. It's why I liked the boxing, too."

He then embarks on another tale concerning another uncle – this time his Uncle Jim.

"Jim's quite fiery," says Derek. "I'm quite a calm fella myself but there must be some gene in the family that gives some of the males a bit of a temper. You'll know what I mean. My brother Paul has it and so does Uncle Jim.

"I remember that I was just seven and I was on my way for my first Holy Communion, walking along the street in my little suit and my polished shoes to the church with Uncle Jim holding my hand. Then along comes a car, straight through a muddy puddle it goes. Well, you can see the picture can't you? Right over me goes all the muck. I can't honestly remember being that bothered myself about a little mud splashing my clothes. But I knew it wasn't what was supposed to happen 'cos Uncle Jim just sort of, well, he just sort of exploded. It was like watching a volcano erupt. It was like one of them angry faces you see in the comics – all red it was with steam shooting out of the ears.

"I remember him shouting: 'I know whose car that is, I know the bastard, I knows where he lives.'

"And we were off. He still had hold of my hand and we was walking so fast that my little legs could hardly keep up and I kept tripping. But he doesn't stop, just keeps lifting me up by the arm and dragging me along.

"Next thing I knows is this fella up against the wall with Uncle Jim's hand round his throat. Jim's pointing at me with his other hand to make his point and he's shouting so loud my ears are busting.

"The other poor fella's spluttering, or maybe he's choking. It's hard to tell when you're just seven. Anyhow, he gets out his wallet and hands me five punts to pay for my suit to be cleaned up and that. I'm stood there with a lovely, crisp fiver in me hand and I tell you what I'd never seen one of them things ever before.

"But before I can even think of all the sweets that I'm going to be buying, Uncle Jim grabs the note out of my fingers and throws it back at your man.

" 'We don't want your dirty money,' he shouts."

It was at that point the young Derek had to hold back those salty tears as he witnessed the cash disappear back into the wallet. He was then taken to church to make his own pledges, being sworn-in as a member of the Holy Catholic family.

An almost cherubic beam breaks across Derek's face as more tales of younger years come to mind.

"My dad's best friend is Willie Wall and he's some character, I can tell you. The pair of them and Johnny, they was always up to something or other."

Derek then tells of the day one of them set off for some early morning hunting. He deliberately declines to mention which one he means.

"He was riding along on one of those Honda 50 motorcycles, with a shotgun strapped to his back. Round a corner he rode and suddenly there in front of him was a horse stood stock-still.

"Your man, he brakes and skids off the road into a ditch

and off goes the gun," says Derek. He jumps off his stool to demonstrate the point.

He pauses, then adds: "Finally he climbs out of the ditch, all bruised he is. It takes a while for him to get back his senses. But then he looks around and his eyes begin to focus. And there in the middle of the road is the poor old horse lying stone dead with a gun-shot through its head."

Derek looks at me.

"And that's a true story," he says, slapping the table as if I might disbelieve him.

And then I realise why I might be expected to disbelieve him – he tells me that his father was once winner of his home town's prestigious 'Biggest Liar Competition.'

"Biggest liar?"

"Yes he was the Biggest Liar winner," says Derek with ill-disguised pride. "He won a bottle of whiskey for it too.

"What you had to do was stand up in the pub and tell everyone a tale," continues Derek.

"This fella had just been telling how he'd caught a 6ft salmon. He was stretching out his arms, you know, like the fishermen do to show everyone just how big that fish of his had been.

"Anyhow, next thing it's my dad's turn and up he stands.

" 'Ach, that's nuttin,' he says. 'I was fishing off the same bridge just the other day it was and after a while I knew it was a big 'un I had. So big it was that I thought I was going to be pulled off the bridge and into the river myself. Then out of the water I reels in a huge, great lantern – made of solid gold, so it was.'

"People in the pub were shaking their heads," says Derek.

"But my dad carries on. 'A beautiful lantern, I'm telling ye. And I'm telling you too there was a candle in that lantern. And the candle was still lit.'

"'Ah sit down will you Pat, that's so not true,' says someone in the pub.

"'Is it not?' says my dad. Well you take three foot off that salmon of yours there, and I'll blow out my candle.'"

And so it went on.

Derek can reel off such stories by the dozen.

Another favourite is his father asking Willie about getting some vegetables for dinner the next day. An easy way was to find a farm and "borrow" a few spuds, greens or whatever from a field.

"Right, I'll meet you there at 7.00 tomorrow morning," says Pat.

"Seven? I don't think so. I'll be there at five. There'll be too long a queue by seven."

And one final one.

"Willie told my dad to phone up this pet shop in Waterford. So my dad does just that, putting on his poshest voice and asks if they're in the business of selling finches and canaries because he's a collector of the birds.

" 'We do, sir,' says the shopkeeper.

" 'Well I'll take the lot,' says Pat. 'I'll be round this evening before you shut.'

"Then it's Willie's turn and a few hours later he's down the shop pretending to be a breeder and he asks the shopkeeper if he'd be interested in buying a few finches.

"Well normally 'no thanks' would have been the answer, I guess, but, of course, they've just had this big order, haven't they? Well, the shopman, with an eye for a nice, tidy profit, takes the birds off Willie's hands for 15 punts each.

"Now, that's a nice piece of business for Willie, don't ye think? He walks away with a nice 90 punts in his pocket."

Derek smiles to himself and explains a little more of his childhood.

"We were always outside," he says again. "Even when we went to discos it meant being outdoors as we had to walk everywhere to get there. There were no taxis or even buses in New Ross at that time, you know.

"You had a car or you walked it. I remember we'd walk the 15 miles or so to Waterford to get to a disco and then have to walk all the way back in the dark. Actually, I liked to run."

One of New Ross's main claims to fame is that it was the ancestral home of former US President John F. Kennedy.

Every other town in the republic might make some such claim, but it is a fact that it was JFK's forebear, Patrick Kennedy, who left the family house seven miles from New Ross and sailed from that port across the Irish Sea to Liverpool. From England he sailed in 1849 to Boston in America.

The population of Ireland in those years was falling rapidly in the midst of unimaginable tragedy. Between 1845 and 1848 more than a million people died in the Great Famine and in a bid to escape the unfolding horror another million left their homeland, many thousands through the port of New Ross.

One of those emigrant ships was the *Dunbrody* built in Quebec and owned by a New Ross family.

A modern-day replica of the ship, which, interestingly, Derek's father helped build, is moored at the quayside in New Ross; a reminder of Ireland's tormented past.

Modern nations, of course, are moulded by their history and Ireland is no exception – the sufferings of past generations are remembered and their struggles revered.

If such a thing as a national psyche exists then Ireland's must surely be one of determination, a determination to battle on – or as Irish writer Roddy Doyle might say, a striving to triumph over adversity.

I say that even though I can almost sense professional historians removing tweed jackets, rolling up their sleeves and reaching for their mightiest of pens to criticise such a statement with phrases like "such a simplistic concept of Irish history..."

So what, I wonder, would they make of my notion that it is just such a battling characteristic that has helped Ireland produce so many fine fighters over the years?

"Well, what do you think, Derek?

"Could be so," nods Derek, sipping again at his Guinness. "Could be so."

The Irish themselves, of course, have a keen sense of their own nation's past. Derek is no exception. His ring name 'The Rebel', is a tribute to a particularly bloody piece of Irish history when poorly armed rebels captured New Ross in 1798 and drove out the defending English troops. The garrison returned, however, and recaptured the town, burning the thatched buildings and slaughtering up to 2,000 rebels. It was an horrific event, marked in the town by a memorial and garden of remembrance.

The New Ross rebellion was a part of the popular rising against English rule in many counties across Ireland at the time. As it happens, two of the rebel leaders in County Wexford were Edward Roche and a battling cleric by the name of Father Phil Roche. Fr Roche was hanged on Wexford Bridge along with eight other resistance leaders on June 25 of 1798.

What ancestry, if any, Derek shares with these Roche heroes of the 18th century he is unable to say, but, perhaps unsurprisingly, Derek cites history as having been among his favourite subjects at school.

He hands me a tape for my research, which I misread as 'The Crappy Boy 1798.' "That's The Croppy Boy 1798," Derek corrects me, shaking his head and possibly wondering if I am the right man for this job. Anyway, it is a compilation of songs, including *The Boys of Wexford*, sung by Ger Busher and I for one would recommend it.

Derek attended St Michael's primary in New Ross from the ages of five to seven before progressing to the local Christian Brothers Junior School to the age of 12. From there he went on to the Christian Brothers Secondary School until leaving when he reached 18.

Now, for the many thousands who have experienced a Christian Brothers' education there are many who can recall tales that conjure up images to make Vlad the Impaler sound slack in the discipline department.

Somewhere along the line, though, the brothers must have done a good job on Derek as he passed his intermediate certificate. His subjects were English, Irish, maths, accountancy, history, economics, geography and French, and all the same subjects, save French, for his leaving certificate – the equivalent of English A-levels.

"That's impressive learning," I tell Derek but he is already embarking on more memories.

"It was strict at school," he recalls. "But it wasn't too bad, to be fair. I remember one teacher who used to strip holly sticks to beat the kids with, but that wasn't one of the brothers, it was a woman teacher.

"And anyway," he smiles, "I was always a good boy."

It is a statement that some boxing opponents since those early days might find a little hard to believe.

"I remember we always had to be smartly turned out for school," says Derek

"I was a bit surprised when I first came to England and saw children at school in trainers and that. We had to wear black, polished shoes, I remember. Very strict they were about that. Times have changed a bit now, I guess. Things aren't as strict as they used to be.

"I went back to my old primary school a while ago to show them the British welterweight belt I'd won and the headmaster introduced me and he must have thought he'd use me to set a good example.

"He said: 'When Derek was here he never went round punching people.' Then one of the boys shouted out 'no he just kicked them.'

"I was a bit surprised by that, I'll tell you. God help anyone who'd spoken out like that in my time. The teachers would have been on them like a ton of bricks."

Derek, though, says he did not fight much outside the boxing ring as a lad.

"It's one of the things you learn as a young boxer, not to use your fists in anger outside the ring. OK you know how to look after yourself but you don't go round picking fights. Apart from anything else you soon learn what damage you can do. Besides which you've nothing much to prove."

I was well impressed.

He added: "Of course, when I went to secondary school and some of the bullies wanted to shove my head down the toilet, I had to knock them out."

He pauses a moment. And then he adds that by the time he was 16 he was involved in a few street fights.

A few?

"Well I suppose it was every night, but only the normal stuff that young lads get up to. And then the Gard came round to see my parents. It all helped to make my mind up that I was going to have to move on and leave New Ross. Looking back I guess I can see I was getting a bit wild. I'd say it was only the boxing that was keeping me in check at all."

Derek had been introduced to boxing at the tender age of eight when his father took him down to one of the two clubs in the town. There was the CBS club and St Michael's.

"I went to St Michael's because my dad was a friend of the trainer, Stan Blanche," says Derek.

Stan was an ex-pro who had plied his trade in Australia and the USA and once fought Italian Rocky Mattioli who went on to become the WBC world light-middleweight champion.

Derek's brother Paul joined the gym too, but, unlike Derek, did not take to boxing and left after a time to join a karate club.

Other lads at the same gym included Stan's nephew Jason Blanche who eventually joined the paid ranks and had about 15 pro fights at light welter. He was a four-times Irish champion at his weight.

There was Sylvie Furlong who went to America and boxed pro. He was to fight Adrian Stone in 1994 in Boston, the boxer Derek later challenged for the IBO world light middleweight title.

"I remember when we were older Stan used to encourage us to think about turning professional," says Derek. "He said 'you've put so much into it, it's about time you got something back.'"

Stan was not wrong when he said the lads had put a lot in and those unfamiliar with the amateur game might be surprised at the physical and mental effort required of lads as they progress.

Amateur trainers are hard taskmasters; they have to be

because they know what huge sacrifices the sport demands. Their skills should not be underestimated either; there are many whose talents match those of the professional coach. The financial rewards for the amateur trainer, though, are pitiful to non-existent, the hours unsocial and the travelling, because amateurs usually compete so frequently, can be exhausting.

"We were all over the place," says Derek. "And remember the roads in Ireland at the time weren't like over here. We came to England too. We boxed in Cardigan, which is in Wales, (perhaps Derek has heard about my geography weakness) we boxed in Reading and we boxed in Coventry.

"The first time I ever went on a train is when I came to England. Travelling about was a big adventure. We had a lot of fun."

The travelling is a weighty responsibility for the amateur trainers on top of all the coaching and, perhaps, it is little wonder that so many often have world-weary faces. They carry on, I guess, because they love the sport and the craic of the gym, compulsory, though it might be for them to shake their heads every so often and grumble: "I don't know why I'm still in this game."

The relationship trainers have with boxers is intense and built on mutual respect and they are also some of the most astute observers of human nature.

Good trainers can usually tell soon after a lad walks into the gym for the first time whether or not the youngster will stick at it. For every lad who visits the gym and progresses past the novice stage there are dozens more who drop out along the way. But the very fact that lads continue to turn up at gyms, regardless of whether or not they stay the course, is evidence of the appeal boxing has among certain youngsters. The wiser politicians and community leaders will recognise the value of the service that clubs provide.

Many lads will go to the gym only a few times. Some may even visit only once. The truth is boxing requires commitment and if the motivation is missing in the first place then there is not a whole lot of point in persevering.

Some youngsters begin to box and even pass their medical

only to quit after a fight or two, disheartened by defeat. The shock and reality of being hit in a sparring bout, let alone a competitive match and the loneliness of the ring is simply too much for many.

"It does take a lot to climb into the ring when you're just a boy," says Derek. "Getting up there in front of a lot of people and then showing what you can do takes a bit of courage, for sure. And it's a different world inside that ring, believe you me. You might have a big crowd shouting but that ring is a lonely place."

The atmosphere enveloping many amateur shows should not be underestimated. Many shows attract spectators in their hundreds, crammed into the concert halls of smoky, working men's clubs or similar venues where the brightly-lit bars can help stoke up the partisan fervour of some spectators. Perhaps, it is little wonder that young, raw amateurs, let alone seasoned seniors, often suffer what actors would call stage fright. Boxing clubs are usually well advised to take their young fighters to a show or two before their debut just to familiarise them with the surroundings they can expect to encounter. Then again, there are those who argue that if a young boxer sees what awaits him before he's even had a bout he might just use his common sense and never turn up when the time to box eventually comes.

Simply arriving at a venue can be intimidating enough, with testosterone so thick in the air you can almost cut it with a knife and sell it in slices. By the time the young novice reaches the changing rooms – that being more often than not a hastily swept back-room bar – the inevitable butterflies flying about the stomach will have turned into vultures tearing away at every imaginable internal organ.

Needless to say, everyone else involved in the evening will seem to be wearing expressions that suggest that it is just yet another day at the office.

The urge to run away and sign up for any other sport – including long-distance swimming even if you cannot swim – is almost overwhelming.

Hardly surprising that so many lads drop out before their careers have time to bud let alone blossom.

For those who stick with boxing, though, as Derek obviously did, the only promise they get is that years of hard toil lie ahead.

That is why it is fair to say, that those who persevere and overcome their reservations are indeed a special breed.

The stage does arrive, though, for most boxers when the main worry about fighting becomes not the crowd and not the pain but those sickening few moments after the final bell when the boxer waits to see whose hand is raised by the referee.

Perhaps it is then a lad can call himself a fighter.

Even for those with a natural ability, and the required nerves of steel, the first bout is just the building block. Fitness, stamina and strength have all to be worked at constantly.

There are hours of pad work and bag work and countless rounds of sparring to perfect punches, combinations, defence and footwork.

To the casual spectator, a boxing contest might appear to be simply two opponents leathering each other for all they are worth. But that is the same as being under the impression that cricket is simply a case of whacking a ball as hard as you can with a big lump of wood.

The intricacies and subtle skills of boxing are easy to miss – but slow down a film of two knowledgeable, well-trained boxers competing and the beauty and artistry of the sport becomes evident even to the untrained eye.

Naturally when youngsters first set out, their initial bouts are usually little more than wild milling as they race out of the corners into the centre of the ring at the bell, firing away with gloves often bigger than their own heads. Neither fighter at this stage will, or should, have progressed past step one of boxing's learning curve.

They fight three minute-and-a-half or three two-minute rounds. That might not seem a long time but only those who have never experienced it would say so. Generally, the two boxers at this stage in their learning stand toe-to-toe for much of the match, swapping straight punches – left-right, left-right, left-right, until the final bell or until one of them is pulled out exhausted.

The joy on the winner's face has to be seen to be believed and for the loser there is at least the consolation of having gained the respect of an appreciative audience. Of course, it is not much consolation at the time but even the defeated will have memories he will never forget.

Derek, himself, first climbed into the competitive ring when he was just eight years old.

He recalls that first ever bout in the black and red colours of St Michael's. "It was at the Phoenix Bar in North End, Wexford," he says. "I boxed Josey Breen and lost on points."

Over the next 10 years Derek had 65 amateur bouts and won about 50. It is an admirable record, particularly bearing in mind that in amateur boxing, the scoring can be subjective and there are some away shows where, to use the old adage, 'you need to knock out your opponent to get a draw.'

Over a period of time though anomalies tend to even themselves out, yet it can be heartbreaking for a young lad to be denied victory in a bout which he feels he has won. Then again, perhaps, that is all part of the learning process too.

In the pro game scoring is no less subjective. At times results are downright puzzling. One tale, hopefully apocryphal, to have done the rounds related to the referee who confided once that when in doubt he would award the professional contest to the fighter displaying the fewest tattoos.

Of Derek's amateur bouts, he says: "I enjoyed nearly all of them. But I remember always wishing there was one more round or two more rounds. At the final bell I'd sometimes be thinking, so is that it?"

It is a significant point for Derek to make because he is a fighter whose natural style is better suited to the professional game than to the amateur bout.

Derek's main strengths in the ring are his stamina and heavy punching, which allow him to wear down opponents and look for a stoppage, or from a victory coming from points largely accrued in the later rounds. In a ten-rounder or an eight-round professional fight, a boxer can afford to bide his time in the earlier rounds, work out his opponent and then pick up the points in later rounds as the opponent tires. It is why Derek prefers the longer fights, he says. Naturally if the opportunity arises to finish it early he will not turn it down.

As they say – you do not get paid overtime.

Boxing was not Derek's only sporting passion as a youngster. He was also a talented hurler.

Now, hurling looks a dangerous sport if for no other reason than handing big sticks to a field full of Irishman might seem to be asking for trouble.

"It can be tough," admits Derek. "Like most things, though, it's a matter of knowing what you're doing."

As a lad, he played in midfield for the town's Geraldine O'Hanran's hurling club. Such was young Roche's proficiency that he was selected for the Wexford county side at Under 14, Under 16 and Under 18 levels and had he stayed in Ireland would more than likely have gone on to greater things in the game with Wexford, recognised one of Ireland's top sides.

"If anything when I was young I preferred the hurling to the boxing," says Derek. "But as I got older that changed. I'm not sure what it was. Hurling's a team sport but in the ring it's just one on one.

"In boxing, you're all by yourself in there once the bell rings. There's no-one else but the other fella there in front of you. What happens is down to yourself. I suppose I like that.

"Whatever I do I'll always try my best. I also guess I maybe thought that one day I could probably make a living out of boxing. You can't do that in hurling. "Anyway when I packed my bags, I left hurling behind. There was no chance of playing it in England."

The decision to leave Ireland was a natural progression.

"When I was growing up everyone was going across to England, most of them heading for London. There was no work in Ireland unless you had a family business or something like that.

"My dad wanted me to go to college but I'd had enough of school by then. He took me to see the careers teacher.

" 'So Derek, what do you want to do in life?' asked the teacher

"I told him: 'I want to be a boxer.' "

It is not hard to imagine the sigh escaping from the teacher like wind being driven out of a wheezing, chalk-filled punch-bag.

Derek's father though was more understanding.

"I'll always remember my dad saying: 'What's wrong with being an educated boxer?' "That sticks in my mind."

But there was to be no persuading Derek.

"My mind was made up. I packed my bags and off I went. I was determined to make a go of it."

Chapter Three

Early mornings and Buster the boxer

THE bedside clock's alarm sounds.

Derek hauls himself out from beneath the covers and prepares for his morning run. Outside, the street lamps reflect on wet flagstones and stain the drizzle on the windows an amber hue. It is 6.00am, a time when the sane still sleep unless jobs force them to heave their weary frames from the comfort of warm beds.

But for men like Derek, boxing is a job. Perhaps they are all a little insane too.

"Listen, if you box you have to put in the roadwork," says Derek in his matter-of-fact manner. "There's no getting away from it. That's what you have to do. And the best time to run is early in the morning before the traffic and the fumes all build up."

Even so the streets of Leeds on a cold, wet, winter morning, when most of the city is still asleep, seem pretty uninviting.

But Derek is adamant: "There's no point in complaining. You get on with it. It's the same for any boxer. No one forces you to be a fighter. It's your own choice."

He waits a moment then emphasises: "I made that choice so I have to do the work. Simple as that."

Derek adds in a lighter tone: "Running's the basis of all fitness, whatever the sport. I'm out running every day when there's a fight coming up; at least three times a week when there's nothing in the pipeline.

He pauses again and then adds: "The only time of year I don't run outside is if it's icy."

It is enough to make icy weather seem attractive, don't you think?

Derek continues: "When it's icy, you might slip and break something."

Very true, I muse.

"So I go and run on one of the machines in the gym instead."

Now, this sort of dedication will be familiar to most athletes, including practically every successful boxer. It is one of the compensations of being a writer and not a fighter.

But maybe if I am honest with myself, perhaps I am a little envious. The idea of being able to run without first having to reserve a ride home in an ambulance has a certain appeal.

So I try to coax out of Derek some insight into the torment of this running lark.

"Once you're up and out, it's enjoyable," he insists. "It clears your head; relaxes you. Some people reckon they do their best thinking when they're out on a run. Anyway, I've always stayed fit between fights, so the running's not a problem.

"When there's a fight coming up, I just step it up a bit to raise that fitness level to a peak.

"At the same time it's possible to over-train, you know, and you'll be worn out by the time the fight comes up. That happened to me in my first two pro fights and it was only my 'heart' that got me through them, that's for sure. It's a matter of getting the balance right.

He adds: "But running is still a vital part of any training programme."

Derek zips himself into his running suit and after a few stretches, steps on to the street outside his house, jogging on the spot as he tightens the strings of his hood. His warm breath condenses in the cold air.

Then he is off towards Harehills Park, the first stage of his eight or so miles.

Derek's usual route takes him past the rows of red-brick terrace houses in his own neighbourhood and into some of the more affluent areas of the city before he arches round, burning up the miles, and eventually reaches what is definitely one of Leeds' swishest districts, Roundhay. A massive park dominates Roundhay with exclusive houses nestling along the tree-lined lanes, home to some of the city's more wealthy residents, including, as it happens, Sir Jimmy Savile.

Into the park and an ideal route for runners encircles the large man-made lake. Sometimes Derek drives to the park and runs around the lake with his dog, Buster. You will not be surprised to learn his dog is a boxer, by breed rather than inclination, that is.

Out of the park, Derek can take a direct line along a main road back towards home, by which time the morning's commuters are beginning to get into their cars.

Roadwork is only a part of a boxer's training programme and there are countless hours in the gym to contend with in preparation for fights. But as Derek says, and most trainers will confirm, the gym is not the place to *get* fit – a fighter needs to already be fit before entering the boxing gym. The gym helps to maintain fitness but its real function is to allow fighters to perfect their moves, sharpen reflexes, learn a whole range of boxing techniques and prepare for a particular opponent.

Now coached by seasoned trainer Terry O'Neill, the gym Derek uses was set up by local amateur trainer and street philosopher Leroy Brown, also known as Sharky. It provides a vital facility for youngsters, as well as a home for the professionals. Located on a busy main road about a mile out of the city centre, it is surrounded by old mills and workshops, some now converted into student accommodation.

It is a tidy gym, well lit and well equipped, itself converted from an office suite.

Naturally, boxing gyms vary and there are some that fit people's preconceived ideas of dimly-lit basements where the same smell of stale sweat and leather seems to have hung in the air for decades like a fetid tribute to hard times.

Over the years, Derek has trained in a variety of places but he insists that it is not so much the gym itself that matters but what goes on within it that is important – and that very much depends on the trainers.

"The best-equipped gym in the world can't produce boxers with a useless coach," he says.

So what makes a great trainer?

"Well, obviously he has to know what he's talking about but apart from that I'd say that a trainer's personality is important," says Derek. "It's like being a good school teacher, he has to able to convey his ideas. Some people can do it, others can't.

"The coach and the boxer have to get on well in the gym because it's a special kind of relationship. They have to understand each other. So there are some trainers who get on better with some kind of boxers than others and vice-versa. It's about getting the best out of each fighter – building on skills and working on weaknesses."

Derek recognises that the amateur coaches are a vital ingredient in the sport as a whole.

He pays tribute to all his own amateur coaches as well as to one he has never been trained by but whom he knows as a man and by reputation – Harry Pinkney.

Harry, who was already in his seventies when Derek was defending his British title, runs Meanwood ABC in Leeds, just a mile up the road from Derek's gym.

"Since I came to Leeds, I've known of Harry and his reputation for turning out some of the best amateur champions around," adds Derek. "I don't know anyone who has less than respect for Harry."

Harry, in fact, has been one of the country's longest serving and most successful boxing coaches, in spite of having suffered the most appalling of tragedies – the death of his own son after a boxing contest.

Michael Pinkney, a Junior ABA champion, made his professional debut at Bradford's Midland Hotel in 1971. He won that fight and also his second at the National Sporting Club HQ in London. Boxing folk from that era remember just what a fine prospect Michael was. But then in just his third professional contest – on February 2 1972, in Bradford – Michael collapsed in the ring and died shortly afterwards. The boxing fraternity in Leeds old enough to remember the tragedy still find it hard to talk about.

A post mortem examination revealed that Michael had died from a vagal inhibition – inhalation of vomit that caused the vagal nerve to fail and the lungs to collapse.

The pathologist stated it could have happened to Michael sitting at home having a drink.

"It was a tragic, freak accident," Harry told me. "I'm sustained in the knowledge that his death had nothing to do with the sport he loved so much. That has given me the strength to carry on in boxing. I'm sure that's what Michael would have wanted."

Derek says: "There're perhaps some people outside the sport who won't be able to understand how Harry could carry on after what happened. I wasn't even born at the time, so obviously I didn't know Michael, but being a boxer myself I feel I know that Harry's right when he says that carrying on in the sport is what Michael would have wanted."

Every gym will have its own way of doing things but the principles remain more or less the same.

Young lads who walk into any boxing gym are first of all taught the basics.

Trainers take the youngsters on to the pads – gloves which the trainer wears and which the boxer punches. First comes the stance and there are the constant reminders to always tuck that chin in. There is the jabbing, and then a whole gamut of shots leading up to combinations.

It might surprise some to know that one of the most common mistakes of newcomers is a tendency to hold their breath when they punch. Clearly, the body needs oxygen, so the new boxer needs to learn to control his breathing.

Even so, the physical agony of the boxing gym is likely to be a shock to most newcomers. The lungs burn, sweat stings the eyes and the arms feel like they have been injected with molten lead.

"And that's just lacing up your boots," laughs Derek.

The bag-work involves hours of practising and strengthening punches. Punching itself is a deceptive art. It looks simple of course, but is not as easy as it appears.

"The power comes up through the body from the toes," says Derek. "Equally important, though, is the timing. It's hard enough to thump a swinging bag effectively but trying to hit a quickly moving target like a trained fighter is something else."

Even if the novice boxer is able to make contact on any part of the opponent's rolling, weaving body it is likely that the opponent will be moving in the same direction as the shot. It means the puncher will be stinging with all the venom of a butterfly.

So why when the opponent then jabs back is it like being hit by a runaway cement wagon?

But young novices should be spared the hurt in early sparring, which usually starts with the youngster being taken around the ring by another more experienced boxer just to get a feel for the squared circle.

That first sparring session, though, can still be intimidating – it is a big step forward.

It is always pleasing to see the early progress made by youngsters over the weeks and seeing their confidence and self-respect grow. It is the initial progress that is usually the quickest and most obvious.

But you cannot run until you can walk. There are many ring skills the novice does not really need to know until he moves up a stage or two. It is better first to master the basics.

Usually a boxer new to the game will have a style that is natural to him – maybe he will be someone who comes forward, guard up and then unloads shots or maybe he will be quick on his feet using the space of the ring to stay out of trouble.

Once contests come around, the boxer has, of course, to be evenly matched so as not to find himself in the ring with someone too experienced (or much bigger).

If you think of a boxer as being a car mechanic then the first step is to provide him with the basic tool kit. The first bouts are like opening a bonnet and having a look at the engine, becoming familiar with the layout. Then it becomes a case of trying out, let's say, an oil change. Eventually the mechanic needs specialist tools for those specialist jobs and for a boxer this means having the necessary abilities to cope with different types of opponents and situations.

By this stage boxing boasts some mathematical qualities too – combination punches are like an equation – a fighter might fire off two shots, three, four or more. It is a matter or reading the situation to know what options are best. On top of all this the fighter needs to remain ever wary of a counter punch.

Boxers need to be able to block, parry, slip and feint.

Many fights are won by first recognising and then taking advantage of an opponent's weakness.

"What you're saying is right," says Derek, "but it's not like you're thinking about it all of the time; you just practise and practise until it's like second nature. The concentration, though, is very intense."

There are dozens of examples of moves to recognise – here is just one: imagine you are boxing a fighter who adopts a low left guard and who is hoping to spring a quick shot; you feint with a dip of the left shoulder, trying to tempt him into throwing the strike. You then step quickly to the right emerging on his now exposed left side and you unload a right shot over the top. If that punch is good enough then your man is going down.

Of course, there are great fighters who do leave their guard low – it is a trademark of Ingle professionals, for example. But it is a style that few coaches elsewhere seem to encourage – after all, not everyone has the reaction speed of a Naseem Hamed, or a Herol Graham. Brendan Ingle would also point out that youngsters at his Wincobank gym in Sheffield are first of all taught to box in orthodox fashion with hands up, then southpaw, again with hands up, and then to learn to switch before developing their own style. Whether or not they have their hands up when they box competitively depends on the range and what works best for them against a particular opponent.

Derek says that it is easy for observers to fail to appreciate that the two men in the ring are both trained boxers – often highly-trained boxers. If one of the competitors was a non-fighter then it would more than likely be a simple case of a straight one-two, wham-bam and that would be that.

I venture that not everyone, particularly those watching on television, appreciates the power of a proper punch. Television tends to sanitise the rawness of most sports even if it manages to capture the elegance.

Derek adds: "The fact is that if a punch is good enough and lands on the right spot then anyone, including a boxer, is going down. But anyone who has never been a fighter is likely to be knocked down by just a softish shot simply because of, I suppose you'd call it the shock. A boxer 'rides' a shot if he can; he recognises the power of a shot, knows what to expect. Even if it wobbles the legs he's got a good chance of being able to force himself on until his strength and senses return. For the non-fighter, the weird sensation of that first wobble is likely to send him over. He'll be on the floor before he knows what's hit him."

Boxers themselves vary; thus you get some fighters with an 'iron chin' while others have the misfortune of having what is sometimes called a 'glass jaw' – a man more easily KOd. It is not easy to know why. Regardless of all his other abilities, a glass-jawed boxer is going to find that boxing never gets any easier.

It is a fact that the abilities of two fighters may cancel each other out. It then becomes a case of each boxer trying to keep the other in check – both waiting for a momentary lapse in concentration by the other; a fleeting second when tiredness makes the mind go walkabout. Perhaps the head pops up or the guard falls and the time comes for the other fighter to strike and land a blow that will at least score a point.

"They say patience is a virtue, don't they?" says Derek.

Concentration though is vital – and its intensity often goes unrecognised by some fans.

There is one main aspect of the sport, though, that cannot

be taught and that is 'heart.' Either you have it or you do not. It is an instinct. It is the will to battle on when you hit what might be called 'the wall.' It is a vague term but every boxer will recognise it – it is a point in a fight when the temptation to quit kicks in, when it is easier just to say "that's enough" but when, instead, the fighter digs deep and has the courage to battle his way through the fog.

The wall can materialise at nearly every level of the fight game but is almost inevitable in a tough 12-round bout that goes the distance. It is why fighters like Derek have the right to call themselves champions.

It is also an aspect of boxing that separates the fight game from most other sports or why, to paraphrase Muhammad Ali, boxing is the sport to which all others aspire.

It is a rough road, then, that the young boxer chooses when he walks into that gym for the first time.

For those who continue, the first weeks turn to months and the months into years.

Whether or not anyone ever gets to be the finished article is a matter of opinion; there is always the next fight, the next challenge, always room for improvement.

And when a fighter is at the peak of his career – then there is only one direction to go.

It is probably also fair to say that that there is no fighter who is invincible. Everyone has his nemesis – another fighter, who, either because of a clash of styles or the ability to exploit one particular weakness on the night, can overcome his opponent. Think of the matches between that famous trio of heavyweights: Ali, Ken Norton and George Foreman. Ali never really mastered Norton (though he won two of their three encounters, the last one very controversially); Norton was blasted away by Foreman and Foreman, of course, was famously outwitted by Ali in their 'Rumble in the Jungle.'

An older but still a well known example that springs to mind of a fighter exploiting one weakness is Max Schmeling's 12th round KO of Joe Louis in 1934. The German took advantage of the 'Brown Bomber's' tendency, at that time, to subconsciously hold his left guard low, a boxing 'flaw' already mentioned. The defeat was avenged, of course; Louis, who had been odds-on favourite to win the first encounter, took his revenge four years later with a first round knock-out in New York.

There are countless other examples of unexpected defeats in all the weight divisions.

Sometimes it is a surprise, bearing all this in mind, how much credence seems to be given to undefeated records when a better reflection is a regard for who fought whom and when. After all what is an undefeated record worth if a fighter has rarely taken on a worthy opponent or always avoided a dangerous rival? Naturally, that does happen, the reasoning being that professional boxing is as much a business as it is a sport. Even so it is those champions whose opponents have not been all hand-picked who stand tallest.

Obviously, boxers are subject to career plans laid down by managers and promoters who are keen to protect their investment but the fighter willing to meet the hardest challenge is always to be admired.

And when Derek says "I'll fight anyone, anywhere, anytime" I know he means it.

It is a sentiment shared by all true warriors and in Derek's case no-one could say that the majority of his fights have not been tough ones.

The trainer's job, needless to say, is to ensure his fighter is in the best shape possible to meet the challenge and to achieve that needs countless hours of hard work.

The kind of fitness required of a decent fighter hardly comes easily. Getting down to the desired weight can be a tale of torment in itself.

Derek has had to stay within sight of his welterweight fighting weight – 10st 7lb – most of his career and that stretches back into his amateur days. He has managed this mainly by maintaining his exercise regime between fights.

Diet, obviously, is also a priority. No fighter needs sponsoring by a pie shop.

"It's mostly common sense," says Derek who adds that he, partner Tracei and their son Teighan eat mostly the same food. "At home we have baked potatoes, porridge, pasta, rice, chicken and plenty of fresh fruit and veg.

He adds with a grin: "Not all at the same meal, you understand.

"Luckily Tracei likes this kind of food too, so it's not a big issue. When there's a fight coming up I get a little bit stricter with my portions.

"I cut out drink completely within a couple of months of a fight. Between fights I sometimes have a jar or two but to be honest, like most boxers, because of the training from an early age, I haven't got a very high tolerance for drinking, so it's usually better to just not bother. Sometimes I think I'm the only sober Irishman in town. I've even spent St Patrick's days just drinking orange juice. And I remember during the football World Cup in South Korea when Ireland were playing I couldn't touch a drop. Everyone else was making up for me though. That's not to say that I don't like a drink when the chance arrives."

And what about smoking?

"Anyone who doesn't recognise that's a no-go area must have missed the plot," says Derek. He adds that one of the worst aspects of his job as a club doorman is the smoky atmosphere.

"I hate that," he says.

But back to the weight issue. As boxers, or for that matter, anyone, edges towards their mid-twenties there is a tendency to put on weight if for no other reason than there is a natural increase in bone density. And that is why boxers, particularly those in the lower weight divisions, are more prone to having to move up a division or more as they get older.

As if to underline the point, just as I came near to finishing this book, Derek announced that he was moving permanently into the light-middleweight division.

Thus I return to this chapter and quote him.

"I've been fighting at welterweight since I was in my teens

and it's getting to the stage now where getting off those last two pounds is weakening me and that's no good. Moving up to 11 stone for fights is much better for me and I feel stronger for it. I feel I've got the power back in my punching."

There might be confusion in that some boxers actually drop down a weight division as their career progresses. But this usually follows the transition from the amateur to professional ranks and in most cases it is down to harder training by the pro fighter, specifically aimed at reaching the minimum poundage possible. Lower weights can also be achieved with diuretic drugs but any fighter going down that path is asking for a whole lot of trouble, one way or another.

Naturally, there is skill involved in being lean as it is vital that a boxer does not weaken himself in the process – that he still has the strength to compete and defend himself. Not surprisingly, it is a task best left to the experienced coach. There are some professional boxers who put on as much as two stones between the pre-fight weigh-in and the time that they climb into the ring. The weight gain is simply rehydration with fluids being taken in by the bucketful.

Still, it always amazes me that men of 6ft 2in or 6ft 3in can come in at cruiserweight, (190lbs) light-heavy (175lbs) or even below – even 6ft featherweights are not unknown. Put them on my own personal regime and they would be wobbling into the ring at a belt-busting 19 stones or more.

Of course, there are some fighters who do come into the heavyweight category simply because they are out of condition, in other words they are more fat than fit – and America boasts more than its fair share of them. But put them in with a true heavyweight, or, indeed, a classy boxer from the lower weight divisions, and sadly they would soon find their lardy backsides bouncing on the canvas.

True though the old adage might be that a good big 'un will invariably beat a good little 'un, the emphasis should always be on the word "good" rather than size.

Roy Jones Jr. is a great example of a smaller fighter capable of beating the big boys by sheer skill. His victory over John Ruiz in Las Vegas in January 2003 to take the WBA heavyweight title demonstrates the point. It is not that Ruiz was poor – just not as good as Jones. Turn back the chapters to much earlier days and Pittsburgh's Harry Grebb is a prime example of a smaller man toppling the big boys. Grebb was world middleweight champion from 1923 to 1926 but often boxed men more than 80 pounds heavier. He once beat up future heavyweight champion Gene Tunney and defeated heavyweight contenders Gunboat Smith and Willie Meehan. He once even took heavyweight Jack Dempsey apart in an exhibition bout.

It is more likely though that the bigger boxer is the man who is going to throw the harder shots but so much still depends on technique and those shots, remember, still have to land.

It is also the case that the bigger men in general absorb shots better, in other words they are harder to knock down, they soak up the punishment.

Perhaps less appreciated among the public, though, is the advantage a heavier man has in clinches, when he leans against his smaller opponent, sapping his energy, and slowly wearing him down.

Not so long ago I was chatting with Jeff Gale who held the Central Area welterweight title back in the 1970s. Jeff quit boxing when he joined Leeds police but in his fighting days had the occasional spar with the fighter who was the best man at his wedding – heavyweight Joe Bugner.

Joe had a habit, when he became tired, of putting his hands on his sparring partner's shoulders and pulling him down.

Jeff said: "I was in a corner one time and I could feel Joe's knees bending and this dead weight crushing me. I just threw a right hard body shot but it landed low."

Jeff had just delivered a dynamite blow to the happy sacks of the man who was to twice fight Ali.

"By the time Joe was back on his feet I was out of the gym, showered and legging it fast down the street," smiled Jeff.

Ultimately, boxers have to strive to achieve the optimum weight to suit their body shape. So it is that Derek, for most of his career, has come in at welterweight, and, more recently, at light-middle. He has had to fight some boxers of around 6ft who are able to make welterweight because of their slighter bone structure.

Fighting taller boxers can be both an advantage and disadvantage – it is a matter of adopting the right style to suit the occasion.

The advantage of being tall is generally having a longer reach and being able to jab and score from a distance. (This is particularly true in the amateur game). If the shorter boxer can slip punches and get inside, that is fight at close quarters, the advantage can turn in his favour.

One of the greatest exponents of this was Mike Tyson in his heyday. At a shade under 6ft he was a short heavyweight by today's colossal standards but once inside an opponent his phenomenal hand speed and power made him awesome.

Later, Lennox Lewis was able to demonstrate the advantage of size against Tyson though admittedly Tyson by then was slower than in his stunning heyday. Lewis used his size advantage, combined with his skill, to overwhelm Tyson from a distance before finishing him off.

All of this simply illustrates to those unfamiliar with boxing gyms the type of thinking that has to go on as fighters prepare for a showdown – it is a lot more complicated than just turning up and whacking a heavy bag for an hour so.

Many competitors from other sports who try boxing training for the first time are begging for mercy by the end of a session – and that is without anyone actually hitting them.

Derek's friend and travelling companion Danny Thornton, came back to the gym after a 12-month absence from the professional ring weighing about 14 stone. Danny, who won a national Junior ABA title while an amateur with the Meanwood club in Leeds, is nearly 5ft 11in, so by man-on-the street standards he did not look particularly fat when he returned to the gym – he looked like a well-built bloke who enjoyed a beer and a curry.

But by boxing standards he had grown, well, let us put it politely, a little portly.

Three months or a little more later and he was back down

to middleweight having gradually shed nearly two-and-a-half stones.

The weight reduction was reached by hard work, a lot of running, skipping and a controlled diet. No short cuts – just dedication and discipline.

Ironically, when Danny made his comeback it was against a man who weighed in at more than two stones heavier.

"Yeah, well that's the boxing game for you," sighed Danny.

The fight only went ahead after a good deal of consultation but Danny gave his opponent the run-around, winning comfortably on points over six rounds. He was still a little ring-rusty and was tagged by a couple of shots but the way he came through it all was a tribute both to himself and to trainer Terry O'Neill.

In the past I had seen Danny stand toe-to-toe with fighters and swap blows but Terry, apart from getting him back to fighting fitness, seemed to have reintroduced Danny to more subtle boxing skills.

Had Danny tried to slug it out on that night he would have lost. Instead he used the ring, kept his distance and unloaded some clever shots from various angles when the chances came.

How many hours Danny had spent skipping in the gym, it was hard to say, but I remember watching him in the gym one evening and finding myself nodding off, lulled to sleep by the hypnotic whirring of the rope.

Skipping is a bit of a boxing cliché, eschewed it seems by many other sportsmen as being too girlie. The truth is that it not only sheds the pounds but helps keep the feet nimble and the feet, of course, are an integral part of boxing.

Cuban boxers, apparently, are introduced to boxing by first of all learning to dance the Salsa. And boxing is a form of dancing – with a lot of hurt thrown in for good measure.

Getting the feet right is essential, not only for mobility but also, as already mentioned, because punching power starts in the feet. The power comes up through the body like a spring, starting in the toes. Any boxer can be taught to punch as best he can but there are those who believe, with some justification, that the true punchers are born and not bred.

Generally, though, all boxers need to be more than just punching machines to progress a long way.

There are fighters who could knock holes in brick walls with their fists but whose defences are phonetically leakier than a Welshman's Sunday lunch.

Mind you, they will usually still go further than those who can block, parry and slip shots until the cows come home but whose punches would hardly bruise the skin on a dish of cold rice pudding.

Nearly every boxer has his strengths and weaknesses. And every time a boxer steps up a league, those qualities and faults are tested further.

But theorising about the craft is all very well – putting those theories into practice is another matter.

For example, there are tried and tested methods for a conventional boxer in dealing with a southpaw, that is a fighter who leads with a right jab. Yet for some right-handed boxers, i.e. those who lead with the left, coping with a southpaw remains a nightmare throughout their career.

It is often a case of making the best of what you have got.

Hopefully, every time a boxer prepares for a contest his trainer has a strategy – how that contest should be fought – and if that is not working then a Plan B is going to be found up the coach's sleeve.

Doubtless, many a journeyman will be chortling through his gum shield at such a suggestion, recognising his trainer is as likely to pull out a white rabbit or bunch of flowers from up his sleeve as a Plan B.

The journeymen, those unsung heroes of the boxing ring, generally have little time for such luxuries.

One tale from a friend, now retired, who plied his trade at the receiving end of the hurt-game, related an occasion when he was in his corner waiting for the first round to start. He had touched gloves in the centre of the ring with his opponent and listened to the ref go through his 'defend-yourselves-at-all-times' routine.

"I was worried by the size of this fella," he admitted. "He were a giant and all muscle, serious material if you know what I mean. I whisper to my trainer: 'So what's the plan?' The trainer looks across to the other corner where the other bloke's banging his gloves together and snarling.

"The trainer then steps out through the ropes, sharpish like, and whispers back to me: 'Er, keep your guard up.' "

All too often journeymen are the butt of jokes among a certain type of fan who looks at records and sees statistics such as: fought 154, won 20, drawn 2. But they remain an essential part of boxing.

Inevitably they vary in quality. The best – men like Leeds-trained Paul Bonson, a former professional rugby league player – are always capable of pulling off a surprise.

Men like Bonson do not go into fights with the intention of losing. Their main priority is to protect themselves, earn another pay-day and be ready for the next one. If the chance to win a bout comes along they are going to take it. Bonson is a good example of someone who has been in with some of the best and some of the worst and caused a few upsets along the way.

Up-and-coming boxers underestimate journeymen at their peril – most journeymen will have been around long enough to have plenty of ring savvy and generally a trick or two ready for the unwary.

Having said all that, the life of a journeyman is not exactly what you would call an easy one, even if it is possible to make a decent living out of the game by taking fights frequently and more often than not at short notice.

Derek like every boxer has fought his share of journeymen over the years.

"It can be frustrating," he says. "Particularly because the contest is likely to be scheduled for just a few rounds. It's hard to look good against some of them."

He recalls his fight against Birmingham's Brian Coleman in September 2000, his first outing after losing his British title six months earlier.

It was a six-threes (six three-minute rounds) at Barnsley and Derek won easily on points.

Considering his ring rust, it was a decent enough display by Derek as he went to work on Coleman but looking back he says he was unhappy with his performance that evening.

"I'm not going to lose sleep over it but I should have dispatched him early on. Mind you, I was unhappy with my training at the time. Things weren't working out in the gym."

More of that later.

The fact remains that journeymen are not usually easy blokes to shift. Their priority is to cover up and not get hurt.

Coleman, who had fought around 150 pro bouts at the time he boxed Derek, for example, had been in with a whole variety of top boxers. He knew his trade well.

"I still should have stopped him," says Derek.

That night in Barnsley was a return to the venue where Derek had lost his British title.

"That didn't bother me. There were no ghosts there. You can't afford to think like that in boxing. You get out there and you do your job wherever you happen to be."

Certainly Derek had looked unfazed as he entered the arena to face Coleman. He marched to the ring to the stirring sound of the skirl of an Irish piper – unless it was the noise from the changing rooms after someone left the showers stuck on scalding.

"What was the tune?" I asked him.

"I've not a clue," Derek replied.

There was a good crowd in the arena, a knowledgeable one too, but it is fair to say the atmosphere was less than electric. The mood and tension at shows vary from venue to venue and depend very much on what kind of bill is on offer.

Derek acknowledged his own supporters before the fight with a raised hand as the usual pre-bout announcements were made. His mood seemed neutral. Another day at the office and down to business.

Derek floored Coleman early on with a right. But to

Coleman's credit, the Midlander hauled himself up. Thereafter Coleman lived up to his durable reputation, covering up better than a granny off to the shops in frosty weather. He hardly threw a shot, giving Derek almost nothing to hit. Had Derek posed less of a threat, Coleman might have unloaded more.

Immediately afterwards Derek said: "I was comfortable. I enjoyed it. The knock down so early, though, was the worst thing I could have done because then he realised the power of my punches and he just covered up."

Mark McCreath, Derek's trainer at the time, said: "Derek started relaxing at the end and he looked a lot better. Derek didn't get hit. That's the name of the game."

In hindsight, the comments of both Derek and Mark possibly provide a clue as to why their partnership was to be so short-lived.

Derek says: "I prefer to fight than box. I can box but, like I say, if it comes to a scrap I find it hard not to just go to war."

It is an attitude that entertains. It is an attitude, though, that trainers might consider a weakness.

In between contests, Derek continues with his gym work – five or six times a week on top of his roadwork.

When 'ticking over', a typical gym session will involve three or four rounds shadow boxing, six rounds on the bags, a few rounds of padwork, skipping and 'belly' work, like sit-ups plus a bit of sparring.

With a fight looming the training is stepped up, with gym visits twice a day.

"The whole tempo changes. There's a lot more body work, hardening up the body and a lot more sparring, sometimes 12 or 15 rounds a session. I use weights too, but just medium weights; boxers can't bulk up too much, obviously."

The value of good sparring cannot be overstated. While 'ticking over', boxers like Derek will spar every other day or so, usually with stablemates, helping to keep each other sharp.

Inevitably, particularly among the less experienced fighters, the desire to impress means there is a danger of sparring sessions turning into a war.

"It's like wanting to be the gym's top dog," says Derek. "But it's doing no-one any good – the idea should be to improve your technique, not to knock someone else out. The sparring ring's not the place for that. A lot of young lads are slow to understand that. Whoever I get in the ring with I want to learn something, even if it's a raw novice I'm sparring with.

"Wars in the gym just age fighters – if you're sparring like that you're going to shorten your career. Some fighters shorten their careers more in the gym than they do in the proper bouts. On the other hand, I'm not all that impressed with gyms that just do body sparring – when no-one targets the head. The trouble with that is that when it comes to the real thing and you get caught you'll be in big trouble. It's a shock to the system. You don't cope with it. I'd say that's where Ryan Rhodes went wrong."

Derek is referring to the gifted Sheffield fighter from the Brendan Ingle camp who took the British light-middleweight title aged just 20. Seen as a golden boy of British boxing, he was famously taken apart and stopped in the third round by Wigan southpaw Lee Blundell at Bethnal Green in 2002.

"I just think you have to use sparring to prepare for everything," says Derek.

When a fight approaches, different sparring partners are brought in.

"Obviously, you'll want to try and find someone who's as near to your opponent as you can find, so if you're going to be fighting a tall southpaw it'll be useful to spar with a tall southpaw before the real thing. It's not rocket science. I've often gone and been a sparring partner for other fellas and then when I've got a fight coming up they'll spar for me. You can get very used to some boxers, though, and you begin to know their styles inside out – what their strengths are and what their weaknesses are. It's like James [Hare] no matter what anyone says, he hasn't suddenly become a hard-hitter even though he's been knocking opponents out. I've sparred with him enough to know. But he's got terrific hand speed and his timing is perfect. That time he put Roman Dzuman down [for the WBF welterweight title], beautiful uppercut, right on the spot so it didn't need a lot of power behind it. First few times I sparred with James, I couldn't get near him to be honest but then after a while you get to know, well, it's like you can predict what's coming. But, hey, don't get me wrong, I think James is a great boxer and it's great to see him doing so well. He deserves it."

Chapter Four

The name game – from The Game Chicken to Kid Bollock

DEREK chose his ring name 'The Rebel' for reasons already explained. And as ring names go, it seems a fitting title for a professional fighter.

It is not everyone, of course, who likes ring names or nicknames, arguing that they reduce the fight game to the level of a circus.

But for boxing journalists and headline writers, at least, they are a boon, allowing a little more variety in stories – when you've used the same name three or four times in a single report, it is handy to have a different reference to fall back on.

There are others too, promoters in particular, who like nicknames, arguing that they add a little extra sprinkling of showbiz razzamataz to the sport. And to their mind, entertainment is ultimately what boxing is all about. It makes money.

Whatever your opinion, it is beyond dispute that ring names have been around a long time, though, admittedly, some of the older ones are beginning to sound a little quaint.

Bristol fighter Jem Belcher, for example, was known as 'Napoleon of the Ring' which is arguably preferable to Henry Pearce who was named 'The Game Chicken.'

A little later came Tom Cannon, nicknamed 'The Great Gun of Windsor' – sadly ironic, perhaps, as he ended his days by shooting himself.

The list is almost endless: there's 'Nonpareil' Jack Dempsey, the Kildare-born world middleweight champion of 1884 to 1891 and heavyweight Jack Dempsey who, of course, was known as the 'Manassa Mauler.'

Incredibly, over the years there have been more than 2,000

fighters, possibly nearer 3,000 if anyone has the inclination to count them, with the name Kid somewhere in their nomenclature. This includes 14 Kid Chocolates and even a Kid Pepsi Cola. There has been a Kid Cowboy a Kid Chicken and, no kidding, even a Kid Bollock. Bollock boxed only once, back in 1922, against a Joe Minskey in Tacoma USA and managed a draw, according to that excellent boxing website: www.boxrec.com.

It is, perhaps, the names that evoke a particular image that stand out in particular: Roberto 'Hands of Stone' Duran or 'Iron' Mike Tyson, for example, or a personal favourite in James 'Lights Out' Toney.

Then there is Rocky Marciano (born Rocco Marchegiano), who even managed to immortalise one of his punches with the nickname 'Suzy Q', as did Henry Cooper with 'Enry's 'Ammer', as well as Swedish world heavyweight champion Ingemar Johansson whose heavy right hand was dubbed 'Ingo's Bingo.'

As it happens, Leeds-born super-bantamweight Carl Johanneson – nephew of Leeds United football hero Albert Johanneson from the Don Revie era – who fights out of New Jersey in the States has, not surprisingly, adopted the title 'Ingemar' as his second name for the ring.

There are many other names or nicknames too good not to pass on, thus we have Thomas 'Hitman' Hearns, Ricky 'Hitman' Hatton; Sugar Ray Robinson, Sugar Ray Leonard, Sugar Shane Moseley and so on.

A little less sweet but still one to savour is Australian-born cruiserweight Chris P. Bacon.

But who would want to change a name like Fidel Castro Smith?

In his fighting days, Brendan Ingle switched Fidel's name to Slugger O'Toole, allegedly to attract the Irish punters.

Sometimes name changes are inevitable, thus Leeds super-featherweight Daniel James, on account of there already being a professional Daniel James in Newmarket, became Jesse James – it is alleged he was always at his best over six rounds. East Anglian light-heavyweight Steve Spartacus is a similar example. Originally called Steve Smith he had to select another name as there was already lightweight Steve Smith boxing in the UK – so he chose instead to be Steve Spartacus because, he says, a medium had once told him he had been a gladiator in a previous life.

Back in Yorkshire, James Hare was given the nickname 'Lord of the Manor' apparently because he lived in a house a bit grander than a terrace, though he still prefers his original nickname 'The Roberttown Rocket.'

In Leeds, promoter Keith Walker encourages boxers to adopt a title and so we have Lee 'Playboy' Murtagh.

Keith also persuaded a former stablemate of Derek's, Ciaran Duffy to become Ciaran 'Diamond' Duffy. Ciaran was none too keen on the new name apparently, until it was pointed out "diamonds are a girl's best friend."

Others in the same stable as Derek, include Danny 'Yorkshire Braveheart' Thornton and Steve 'Tommy Gun' Tuck. And then there is Pinky Burton, though Pinky insists that is his real name – and you would not want to argue.

As trainer Terry O'Neill says: "With a name like Pinky you need to know how to fight."

In his amateur days, Terry, now also Derek's trainer, was a coach to Stepney-born Terry Petersen (who was later to turn professional) and Petersen can boast that he once fought Mick (though not Mike) Tyson as well as more bizarrely a certain Des O'Connor. Then again, Derek's co-manager, John Celebanski, in his fighting days as a heavyweight, once boxed a certain Tony Blackburn.

Fascinating or not as names might be, you have to admire Steve Holdsworth, who commentates for British Eurosport, on the way he manages to pronounce the names of some of the competitors in matches from the continent. And I can sympathise – writing on Leeds-based Steve Conway's fight in 2002 for the British super featherweight title against Scotland's Alex Arthur, I had to have a lie down after checking the spelling on some of Arthur's previous opponents: Dimitri

Gorodetsky, Alexei Slyachin, Vladimir Borov, Dariusz Snarski, Nikolai Eremeev and Pavel Potopko. And Arthur had only had 12 paid starts.

By comparison anyone would be happy enough to write 'Rebel Roche' now and again.

One grumble might be that every other time Derek prepares for a fight, the newspapers seem unable to resist the headline 'Rebel with a Cause.'

Mind you, that is nothing to get too worked up about; as one sub-editor once said after admitting to having incorrectly spelt Armageddon in a huge front page headline: "Hey, it's not like it's the end of the world."

Chapter Five

Bouncing in Bournemouth

HAVING left school, it was only a short time before Derek decided it was time to move on – to leave New Ross and try his luck elsewhere.

As he sailed on the ferry to a new life in England he knew there was no turning back.

"The main thing in my mind was to prove I could do this. I was only 18, remember. All the way over I was thinking about the conversations I'd had with people back home. They'd been saying things like 'See you in a few weeks, then Derek.' Or 'You'll be back soon enough. I'll give you six months.'

"I knew that most of them meant it well and I knew I was going to miss the family but, at the same time, I felt like I had something to prove.

"Anyhow, there was no work back home."

Like so many of his countrymen, Derek headed first to London.

"I hadn't any clear idea what I was going to do, to be honest, but London just seemed the obvious place to go."

Derek soon discovered the streets of the English capital were not paved with gold – litter and despair, perhaps – but no gold for a young Irishman with little clear idea in his mind of the future, save a vague notion of pursuing a career as a professional fighter.

"I just had a look around for a little while but to be honest I wasn't all that keen on London and I just thought to myself: 'well, I'll be off then.'

"I was going to see my brother Paul in Bournemouth at some stage anyhow, so I decided to go and pay him a visit."

It was not to be the shortest of visits. Bournemouth was to become Derek's home for the next two years.

Arriving on the English south coast, Derek stayed with

Paul, who was sharing a house with two others, including another New Ross man and when Paul moved out Derek took over his vacated room.

"I've got to say I loved it in Bournemouth," said Derek. "It was a great place, especially for a teenager – there were parties and always something happening, always a lot of fun.

"We'd go down to the seafront and there'd be loads of people drinking outside the pubs like the Lord Nelson and Jolly Sailor. There was always plenty of life and something to do. The girls loved the Irish accent too. There weren't too many of us around down there so we were a bit of a novelty and could use the old Irish charm if you know what I mean?"

It was to be boxing, though, that gave Derek a foothold and a start.

He joined nearby Poole ABC, where the trainer was Derek Grant, and it was the coach who offered the young Roche some work as a landscape gardener.

"I'd not done it before but I enjoyed it and it helped keep me fit too. We were doing all the stuff, you know, drives, fences, whatever came along."

He kept up the gym work as well and was soon boxing for Poole ABC, including a bout against Glenn Catley, who was to become WBC super-middleweight champion in later years.

"I had about 12 or 13 fights for Poole in my two years there, if I remember right," said Derek. "I had to get a couple of buses to get there, so I must have been dedicated. And then we sometimes had to put the ring up and the bags because we shared the hall with other organisations and we didn't have all that long for training. But it was a friendly club and there was some good lads down there."

It was also through the club that Derek eventually found himself some extra employment in addition to the landscape work.

"One of the lads came up to me – he'd been watching me box and that – and he asked me if I'd ever done any door work."

Derek breaks off at this point, scratches his head and smiles.

"To be honest, I wasn't sure what he was talking about. I thought he meant hanging doors up or something, screwing them on to the frames and that kind of thing. 'Do you fancy a go,' said your man. I said, 'Well OK' but I was still wondering if I'd need my own screwdriver. Eventually, of course, I caught on what he was on about. I still said 'OK, I'll give it a go.'"

And so Derek's career as a bouncer began.

It was to be the start of an eventful time for young Roche as he was assigned to Bournemouth's Bacchus bar on Christ Church Road where he met a man who was to feature in several eventful moments in his life – a Serbian by the name of Veljko Cerevic.

His pals, of course, all call him Velcro.

"The name just seems to have stuck," jokes Derek.

Veljko, built like a mule, has the kind of east European features that betray few emotions, even though he smiles a lot. The first thing I noticed when we were introduced in Leeds was his handshake which, without being aggressive, leaves you with the impression that, if he wanted, he could tear off your arm and eat it cold for breakfast the next day.

Derek shook his head in disagreement.

"No, he'd not do that," he said. "He could break your thumbs, easy enough, though."

And Derek demonstrated to me how it was done – thankfully without actually having to bust my thumb in the process.

So it was that Derek found himself working alongside Veljko for a local security firm in what might most kindly be described as having been one of Bournemouth's less glamorous night spots.

A welterweight, and not much more than 5ft 9in, Derek obviously falls into the smaller category of doormen.

But at this point it might be worth passing on a bit of, er, advice or just an observation to lager-louts, bar-bums or anyone touched by the old doo-lally stick, and that is there are better ways to enjoy a night out than messing with doormen. It usually ends in tears and normally not theirs. Equally good advice might be to be particularly wary of the smaller doormen – they are not just there for decoration and security firms rarely recruit at Toys R Us.

"You know, I'm not a naturally violent person," says Derek. "I wouldn't want people to be thinking that. Like I've said already there are others in the family who are a lot more fiery than myself. Like my brother Paul. Now, I'll tell you Paul's wilder than myself.

"I remember him getting into a fight one night. This was in Bournemouth. Anyhow, it got split up or whatever and Paul and the fella he was fighting, they say that they'll finish the scrap later. Anyhow because it's late and the bloke can't get home and he's had a few drinks, Paul says he can sleep on the sofa at our place. That's OK and then in the morning up gets our Paul. He's set the alarm for 7.30 and he goes to get the other fella up too. 'Right, he says, you, outside, we're going to finish that fight.' "

Derek shakes his head. "And out they went. Paul won, if I remember right," adds Derek, seemingly as an afterthought.

"Like I said I'm not a violent type myself. But when you work the doors, things happen, because believe me there's some odd people out there, especially when they've had a drink or two."

Things, certainly, seemed to have happened at the Bacchus.

"It was the darkest pub I've ever known," said Derek. "Especially in the downstairs bar. The other thing I remember about the place was the floors were always sticky. It was like having glue on the sole of your shoes. You could actually hear your feet sort of squelching as you walked around."

I wondered what the clientele was like.

"Er, they were mostly goths, bikers, those sort of people and a few regulars with names like Mad Alan.

"Ha, I remember Mad Alan," laughs Derek, as if a picture has just sprung up in his mind. "I don't know if his name was really Alan but, jeez he was mad, for sure. Mad as a box of frogs, he was.

"I was once outside the bar and saw him get out of a cab. He saw me and, I don't know why but he'd decided he was going to have a fight or something that night, like he sometimes did. So off he comes at me, mad as normal. It was quite cold and I had my hands in my pockets so I just lifts up my foot up as he runs at me, not to kick him, mind, just to stop him."

Derek stands up to demonstrate his actions.

"Anyhow, he runs into my foot at full tilt and he bounces back into the road. He's on his back. He's just lying there in the road. Then along comes a lorry and, I'm not joking, it misses his head by no more than an inch."

On another occasion a punter was knocked out cold as he attacked Derek.

"Veljko and me sat him up outside. Five minutes later he was still there and I thought, 'ah jeez, I've killed him.' I was worried, I'll tell you. We went back inside and I got some water and went down to splash it on your man's face. He began to come round and we brushed him down. I was relieved as hell, I'll tell you.

"Anyway we patted him on the back and waved him off, glad to see the back of him, we were."

Five or ten minutes later, though, Derek and Veljko saw the man walking back towards them from the opposite direction.

"Aw no, here we go again, I thought," said Derek.

Apparently, though, the man had shuffled his way around the block in a full circle before arriving back at the Bacchus. He recognised neither Derek nor Veljko from the earlier incident and began to tell them how he'd just been in a fight with a bouncer at some other bar down the road.

And then he boasted: "I gave him a real pasting."

Derek, however, had already been introduced to the harsh reality of working the doors in his first week at the Bacchus.

His first night ended with a KO and it was not Derek on the floor.

He remembers, too, the first customer he was forced to bar.

And so he should – it was his father.

"He was over here to see me boxing," said Derek.

"The next night he came down for a drink at the Bacchus. Just to see where I was working. Anyway this bloke, I won't name him, but he was a twat, let's put it like that. He was winding the ol' man up calling him Paddy this and Paddy that and that's not because he knew my dad's name. Well, my dad's a patient sort but his fuse can go, you know, and suddenly he decides he's had enough and grabs your man and he's all over him. Well, it's my job to pull him off. Then it's outside with the ol' man and I had to say: 'Sorry dad, you're barred.'

"Off he went muttering, I remember."

Derek smiles. "But he didn't hold it against me. He could see the funny side, later."

There was more serious trouble around the corner in that first week, however.

"I think it was my third night or so at the Bacchus and as Veljko and me arrived we knew there was going to be trouble just from the noise inside as we walked along the road.

"We went through the doors and I'm telling ye, it was like the Wild West in there.

"There was a team of rugby players in celebrating after their game. Big, big fellas they were too. Half of them were on the tables, beer slopping all over the place and fellas hanging off the ceiling. They were singing, shouting, pushing, shoving. You know the scene. And I thinks: 'Oh shite.'

"We called the firm for back up, like, but before any of our lads turned up it all kicked off. We were trying to calm things down, you know, 'come on now lads off the tables, will ye?'

"Then a fist flew out of nowhere from one of them. It was just me and Veljko against these massive blokes.

"I remember putting three or four of them down and I was trying to pick my punches as they came at me. All on the chins, one, two, three.

"Then a pack of them all rushed Veljko and he went flying. He crashed out through the front windows. Glass all over the street, there was, and he's just laying there with great big pieces of glass sticking up through his legs. Jeez, there was blood everywhere.

"I was still trying to hold my own and we got outside. I remember then being pulled to the ground just by the sheer number of them. They were on top of me and one of my arms got pinned down under my body and I just couldn't break free."

Derek stops for a moment as if picturing the scene in his mind again. "I looked up and I remember I just saw the bottom of this boot flying into my face. Whack"

Derek pauses again.

And then what happened?

He looks a little puzzled.

"No that was it. The police comes and the ambulance, of course. Poor old Veljko had to have a few operations because he'd lost so much blood.

"And the doctors checked my eyes to see if I was OK after the kicking."

Anyone arrested?

"No, there wasn't really much to say. We didn't know the fellas and that was it."

So did you ever go back to the pub?

"Sure, I did. I went back to work there soon as I'd mended. Carry on regardless – that's my motto."

Derek's scrapes were not restricted just to working the doors, though. Between work and boxing there were parties and fun.

"I guess I was a bit wild in those days. I've calmed down a lot as I've grown up, you know. But, we were young lads having a good time. Nothing bad just the usual sort of thing."

Among the usual sort of things was a party he and another Irish friend attended along with Veljko.

It was a bit of a sombre affair but livened up after a few wrong words. Most of the other partygoers were Royal Marines back home after a tour of duty in Belfast.

An Irishman was not, perhaps, their idea of the ideal party guest and once Derek and his New Ross pal opened their mouths it was a pretty good bet that playing charades was not going to be the highlight of the evening.

"You'd have been cleaning up with a shovel after that one," said Derek. "There was no furniture left by the time we fought our way out. Mind you, we left with more beer than we'd brought."

There was another occasion when Derek and Veljko arrived at the sea-front for a drink at the Jolly Sailor and saw the landlord being set on outside by half-a-dozen travellers.

"Well we knew the fella, so in we waded to help him out. I knocked one of the blokes down straight off but then got grabbed from behind by this big bloke who had me in a headlock. He'll have been about 17 stone or so and was just too strong and I couldn't get out of his grip.

So I shouted out 'watch it the police is here.'

"Well, he looks up and lets his grip loose. I slip out and hit him with a real belting right on his chin that lifts him off his feet.

"The landlord's taken a bit of a kicking by now but he's up off the floor and runs off to lock himself inside the pub. He makes it back inside and starts to shut the door. We run after him to get away and I just manage to get in and Veljko's halfway in when the gypsies grab him by the legs. I get him by the arms and we're tugging each way, me trying to get him in and the gypsies trying to get him out.

"Then I looks down and I sees Veljko's laughing his head off. 'Whatever you do Derek, don't let go now.' He's laughing.

Derek himself laughs at the memory.

"Anyway a few minutes later the lads from our agency arrive from another pub and the gypsy boys leg it. The landlord needed a few stitches in his mouth afterwards but he was OK otherwise."

Much as Derek enjoyed his time in Bournemouth, there was always a nagging feeling that he wanted to be a pro boxer. To do that, he felt he would have to move elsewhere.

"I'd nothing definite in my mind and just carried on with what I was doing. But I guess I was getting itchy feet.

"Then one day I just woke up and thought: 'right, that's it, it's time to move on.'

"It was a spur of the moment thing, really. I packed my two bags, put the few pounds I had left into my pocket and off I went."

Derek decided to head for Leeds more than 300 miles away, simply because it was a big city and one of his friends had married a Yorkshire girl and was living up there.

The couple had told Derek he could spend a few days at their home in Leeds if ever he wanted. He had also been told there were good boxing gyms to be found in the city.

And so Derek bought himself a one-way coach ticket and headed north.

Chapter Six

Hard times in Leeds

LEEDS was, and is, a proud city. Its famous, huge, dome-topped Town Hall stands as a monument to its self-esteem.

But for decades the Town Hall, like the city's other stone buildings, wore a mantle of soot – a black testament to the toil of thousands – a coating of grime from the chimneys that belched out smoke from the coal fires of industry and the countless terraces of Victorian, brick-built homes.

But the face of inner-city Leeds has slowly changed.

In the sixties, concrete was king and acres of the terraced housing made way for high-rise flats and new roads began to snake their way through tight-knit neighbourhoods.

Then came another revolution. The soot from buildings like the Town Hall was sandblasted away. Shopping malls and pedestrian precincts were built and in the 1990s there was another monumental building constructed, which became known locally as 'The Kremlin.' This monolith of Stalinesque proportions dominates the eastern edge of the city centre near to where Europe's largest housing complex, known as Quarry Hill Flats, once stood. The flats, which were home to thousands, once featured in an old TV sitcom called *Queenie's Castle*, starring Diana Dors. But all that seems a long time ago.

'The Kremlin' is a reflection of the new look Leeds and was built to house the offices of hundreds of civil servants from London. The influx created a fiscal catalyst, so they say.

Suddenly, it actually seemed like overnight, Leeds awoke to find it had a new reputation as a boom city, boasting a thriving banking and business community.

Its leaders tagged the city 'the shopping centre of the North.' Even that purveyor of plenty to the poshest of the posh, Harvey Nichols, opened a store in the city – its first outside London. (There was wry amusement when its first shoplifter was brought before the courts to be charged with stealing goods to a value of £100 – a couple or so pairs of underpants, as it turned out).

There was talk of café society. Wine bars and bistros replaced old city centre pubs, mills were converted into swish apartments or offices, house prices in many areas soared, particularly those in the northern part of the city.

Leeds also discovered that its universities had become two of the most popular in Britain, attracting thousands of Home Counties accents, perhaps lured north by Leeds' vibrant night-life reputation.

Yet despite the gloss, Leeds had changed rather less than might be imagined.

While the city centre gives the impression of a thriving metropolis it rubs shoulders with areas largely untouched by this new-found wealth.

There are vast areas of the city where jobs are few, street crime is high and poverty is rife. Life is hard for many people, particularly older members of the community, on the estates and in the rows of brick terraces and in the high rise flats.

It was into this world that Derek arrived in 1993 as he climbed off the coach and went in search of his two friends living in Harehills.

"When I arrived in Leeds, it seemed pretty depressing, to be honest. It was only the second time I'd been to the north of England and Leeds was a big, hostile place after Bournemouth. It seemed a million miles from New Ross and that's for sure."

But there was worse to come.

Derek had been in Leeds only a few days and had hardly had time to find his bearings when the house he was staying in was burgled.

Derek had been out with his friend for a quick drink one evening and they returned home to find the break-in. Derek's two bags containing all his possessions had gone. Doubtless the contents of both had been traded to pay for some smack-head's quick fix.

"I stood in this bare room and couldn't believe it. All I had left were the clothes I was stood up in and a few pence in my pocket," says Derek. "I felt like bursting into tears, to be honest. I just stood there in the room, rooted to the spot. I'd got nothing. It was the lowest point in my life. I had no money, no home and no real friends nearby. You might say I felt a little more than downhearted."

His deep feeling of loneliness, though, was to be emphasised soon after.

His parents sent him a little money over from Ireland so that Derek could at least have a few pounds to help celebrate what was to be his 21st birthday.

It was not the joyous anniversary it should have been, though. Having no-one to share his big day with underlined his isolation.

"It was a pretty depressing time," admits Derek. "I even feel a bit sorry for myself now when I think back on it. I spent my 21st birthday by myself, watching the television. I guess it was a low point. I guess too that I was tempted just to pack it all up and head home to Ireland. But deep down I knew in myself I couldn't do that. Perhaps, it was pride, I don't know. I'd made my bed, as they say. It was up to me to sort it out."

Chapter Seven

Leeds' Irish legacy and settling down

.

IN coming to Leeds, Derek had travelled a path followed by many Irish over the past two centuries. First to come to the city had been the navvies, whose sweat and muscle had carved out the region's canals and railways with pick and shovel.

Families of weavers then arrived in Yorkshire's towns in the 1820s after Ireland's own textile trade declined. This followed the protective tariff on the import of English textiles into Ireland being scrapped.

In Leeds, a community of Irish emigrants began to grow in an area of the city known as 'The Bank' – an area roughly bounded by the Leeds-Selby rail line and the River Aire that winds its way down from the Pennines. The district sits to the east of what is now the city centre. In those more innocent days it was known in local rhyming slang as 'The Ham Shank.' The Bank was made up of hundreds of cramped brick-built houses thrown up in the late 17th and early 18th centuries as England rapidly transformed from an agrarian society to an industrial one.

What was at first a trickle of Irish immigrants turned into a flood in 1847. That was the Black Year when a famine of such proportions hit Ireland that there were genuine fears that it might wipe out the entire population.

The potato was the staple food of Ireland and the crops were rotting in the fields, attacked by *phytophthora infestans* – the potato blight.

The blight, of course, had hit other European countries. But in no other land was the population so reliant on one crop – three million Irish ate nothing but potatoes. This monoculture had grown out of a need to support whole families on tiny plots of land – a consequence of a system of society imposed by Ireland's English landlords.

The potato blight first hit Ireland in 1845, wiping out about a third of the crop. British Prime Minister Sir Robert Peel immediately launched a scheme of public works and spent £100,000 on imported corn from America. (But as A.N. Wilson points out in his book *The Victorians*, seven years later the British Government found £70 million to finance the Crimean War.) Nevertheless Peel's sympathies were in contrast to those of his successor Lord John Russell whose Whig government came to power in 1846. In that year the potato blight struck harder with three-quarters of the Irish crop being lost. But such were the laissez-faire economic policies of Russell's party that the problems were deemed to be the concern not of the government but of the landowners. The irony that many in the government also held vast tracts of Irish lands seems to have been lost on the aristocrats. Foreign Secretary Lord Palmerston, for example, who owned many acres in Sligo, sent no relief to his starving tenants.

In a part of the country close to Derek's hometown, in Dungarvan, County Waterford, the First Royal Dragoon Guards fired on a starving crowd of stone-throwers, killing two and wounding others.

By 1847 a desperate population had already eaten most of the remaining seed potatoes and so very little had been planted. The crisis was at its height.

It must have been hard to believe then, but today it is almost impossible to imagine the scale of the misery and suffering endured by millions as the tragedy unfolded.

In a desperate bid for survival, whole families fled their native country. Many came to Leeds from the western counties of Mayo and Sligo seeking relatives, friends and acquaintances from their homeland villages and towns.

It was soon not uncommon to find three or more families sharing one small house.

In the letters and memoirs of a Leeds Anglican vicar, the Rev Edward Jackson, there are heartbreaking accounts of the scenes he witnessed.

"It was the year of the Irish Famine and as the awful visitation

began to press the poor peasantry in their own country, such as were able to do so, fled to England, to seek among us a morsel of bread.

"Our town from its proximity to the west coast (of England) soon had numerous arrivals of these gaunt, hungered creatures.

"Tall men, with long coats... and women, wild and haggard with numbers of unearthly looking children – strange beings that ran alongside the men and women and looked at you out of the corner of their eyes, with a sort of half-frightened, half-savage expression."

But the authorities in Leeds watched with alarm, rather than pity, at the growing number of Irish poor making their way into the town.

Many Irishmen, women and whole families had, of course, left for America in a bid to build a better life across the ocean. Many came to English cities, such as Leeds and Liverpool, hoping to earn the money to continue their journey. Many, though, realised there was little hope of ever getting to America and those who survived settled permanently in England.

Leeds was an obvious destination, with an already established Irish community providing the new emigres with at least familiar voices, lodgings and the possibility of advice on where best to find work.

Many Irish families though were victims of typhus, or Famine Fever as it was known at the time.

The now defunct *Leeds Mercury* reported that there had been poverty and illness long before the great famine.

Even when work had been found, wages were so low that no matter how many hours men laboured they could not earn enough to support their families properly.

The poor living conditions of Irish families had come to public notice during a cholera epidemic back in 1832.

A report to the Leeds Board of Health, by Medical Officer, Robert Baker, at the end of the epidemic illustrates his concerns over poor housing, overcrowding, the lack of poor drainage and sanitation.

The 1841 Census records 42 dwellings in Boot and Shoe Yard, behind Kirkgate, housing 336 people, and almost all were Irish born. There was no water supply. The piggery at the end of the yard was rented out at a higher rate than the two-roomed cottages.

Nothing seems to have been done by the authorities to upgrade the accommodation, but even in those days it seems there were spin-doctors on hand to fudge the issue – the location's name was simply changed to Richmond Court.

There were just over 5,000 Irish people recorded in the township of Leeds in 1841 – a little less than six per cent of the population. They were mainly concentrated in the eastern wards.

So there had already been an established Irish community before the arrival of many more families fleeing the potato famine.

When the great influx came, the town's authorities did little to help, there was no provision for their needs and the majority were left to find their own accommodation – in lodging houses or with friends and family originally from their own parishes back in Ireland.

The last resort was the dreaded workhouse, an institution based on the Victorian principle that the poor were responsible for their own plight.

Meanwhile countless numbers died in dark, damp cellars and overcrowded attics.

It might be wondered how communities could bear such suffering and yet survive.

But survive they did.

Hardship and suffering, almost unimaginable by today's standards, continued, although as the decades passed there were slow but definite improvements. Over the next century and a half or so, the Irish community has grown, spread and thrived in Leeds and has left an indelible print on the city.

The Catholic churches and schools, the clubs, the associations and the pubs are all a reflection of, and a tribute to, a resilient community that has persevered through tougher times and prejudice. Matters may not yet be perfect, of course, but the progress made is undeniable.

The Irish have brought with them a vitality and culture that has added greatly to life in Leeds. Many families, of course, go back generations and while proud of their Yorkshire heritage they still cling to those Gaelic roots and new arrivals help keep alive the link with the old country.

One of those new arrivals, of course, was Derek, though he hailed from the county of Wexford rather than from the west coast counties where most of Leeds' Irish population originated. Nevertheless Derek was to become a well-known figure among the city's Irish community.

Derek's own arrival in the city was hardly auspicious but once again it was boxing that came to his aid. He had joined Burmantofts ABC soon after he came to Leeds and after the burglary which left the young Irishman with next to nothing, the lads down at the gym were able to loan Derek some spare clothes and help him out.

It was also through the gym that Derek was eventually introduced to Joe Delaney, a man who was to have a pivotal influence on his boxing career.

Slowly Derek became more familiar with the city of Leeds. He was impressed by the city centre itself and came to regard Harehills, and its surrounding areas like Burmantofts and Chapeltown, more as home than a hostile environment.

It is in such areas of the city that the true Leeds lives on. Baseball caps may have replaced the flat caps but the city's diverse, yet distinctive, character continues.

Sporting heroes are deemed above the politicians and other policy makers.

Football is a passion – in Burmantofts even some of the high-rise flats are painted in the blue, white and yellow of Leeds United. And the favourite players, of course, are local.

Rugby League is a source of much pride too, carrying on despite indifference in the south and producing gritty heroes by the dozen.

And then, of course, there is that hardest sport of all – boxing.

Again in Burmantofts, a pub, aptly named the Sportsman, has an inspiring picture of world title challenger Crawford

Ashley hanging outside in tribute. Dreadlocked, he stares down the road, his gloved fists leaving any visitor who might stray into the area in no doubt they are in alien territory.

It is areas like Burmantofts that provide the bedrock of boxing in the city. Burmantofts ABC is sited in the social club just across the road from North Leeds Working Men's Club where the ex-boxers hold their monthly meetings and where they held their 50th anniversary gala. Within easy distance are other amateur establishments – Meanwood, Sharkey's, Star, Bateson's, Hunslet.

All these clubs provide facilities for youths and a distraction from the street crime and drugs that blight many areas of the city.

It has to be said the dedication and hard work of the trainers and club officials all too often go ignored by those elsewhere in authority who seem unwilling to acknowledge the benefits that boxing brings to the communities they serve.

Yet the clubs, despite disapproval from some quarters, continue instilling in the youngsters a sense of value and self-discipline.

They help them learn to survive.

Respect is a key word.

The gyms encourage equality too, stripping away old prejudices. In boxing, race, colour and creed are less of an issue than in many other organisations. Of course, it would be nice to have written "never an issue", but nothing is that perfect.

For all the amateur champions and future professionals the clubs produce there are many more youngsters who sample the sport for only a short time but still take away with them valuable lessons in life.

In the Burmantofts gym hangs the poem for boxers that reads:

Boxing is a science.
The study of a lifetime.
You may exhaust yourself but never your subject.
It is a contest, a duel, calling for skill and self-control.

It is a test of temper, a trial of honour, a developer of character.
It affords the chance to play the man and act the gentleman.
It provides not only physical health but a natural force.
It includes companionship with friends and opportunities to excel.
So go to it you would-be champions.
And may you enjoy every moment of your chosen sport.
But remember we cannot all be champions.

That last line is a worthy sentiment, if a little ironic that Burmantofts should have helped to mould such champions as Crawford Ashley and Derek Roche, and, more recently, Carl Johanneson.

When Derek first arrived at Burmantofts ABC, Crawford Ashley had already embarked on a professional career and was challenging for a WBA world title in Memphis against American Michael Nunn.

Chapter Eight

Paid debut and the
£100,000 challenge

DEREK had just three bouts as an amateur with Burmantofts. The opener was a tough one against soutpaw Lee Murtagh, a Leeds boxer of Irish stock. It was Derek's first fight for 18 months – his first since leaving Bournemouth and he lost on points at the Leeds Irish Centre.

It was not a significant loss in Derek's mind but one that was to return to haunt him in later years when local rivalries emerged after both he and Lee had joined the professional ranks.

"Three rounds just weren't enough," said Derek of that bout. "It made me think more and more about turning pro. Then again I still didn't feel I was ready for it."

The man who was to change his mind was Joe Delaney.

One of the boxers at Burmantofts, Roy Morris, was a doorman at Joe's club – and he took Derek there to meet his fellow Irishman.

"We hit it off pretty quickly and I used to go in and have a drink and a chat with Joe. After a while Roy moved on and then Joe offered me the vacancy on the doors.

Joe, born in Borris in Ossory in County Laois, had come to England in the early sixties "in search of a better future" as he says.

He took various jobs and lived in Birmingham and Manchester before eventually settling in Leeds, first as licensee at the old Prince Arthur pub in the Sheepscar district of the city. By 1985 he'd moved a half-mile or so up the road, establishing Delaney's Bar in what had been a former first-floor snooker hall.

Apart from the bar, Joe has other business interests and had built his business success in part by grasping opportunities when they came along. It was this ethos he passed on to Derek, persuading him that there was no time like the present to turn professional.

Joe took advice from British Boxing Board of Control official Alan Alster, who also happens to be treasurer of the Leeds Ex-Boxers' Association, and Derek was introduced to Bradford-based boxing manager John Celebanski.

Derek was then teamed up with trainer Ricky Manners, whose two brothers Nick and Colin were both Leeds professionals. Joe became Derek's boxing sponsor with John Celebanski as manager.

John is one of those larger-than-life characters; a big amiable man with a true boxer's face.

He got into boxing management and promoting from his base in Bradford after finally hanging up his own gloves.

Among the first fighters on his books was three-times British super-featherweight champion John Doherty from Bradford.

There's another notable John to mention too – John L. Gardner, the former British, Commonwealth and European heavyweight champion whom Celebanski twice took on in his fighting days. Another of his notable opponents was Dave Parris, later to become a Class A Star referee.

Celebanski was also an international amateur whose debut for England happened to be against Poland. That was a mite unfortunate as he says his Polish-born mum refused to speak to him for a few days afterwards.

For some reason it had never occurred to me that John himself could speak fluent Polish until the day he took me to interview a Polish boxer, Adam Zadworny, who had just lost to Derek in Yorkshire.

John had offered to act as an interpreter and we sat in the changing room with the disappointed fighter and his trainer. I asked a question – a pretty useless one, you might not be surprised to learn, something along the lines of: "how do you feel?"

Well, how should the poor lad be expected to feel? He had

just been knocked about, and was beginning to hurt like hell.

Anyhow, John translated whatever it was I asked into Polish. He waited for a response and then turned back to me and gave me the reply... in Polish.

The boxer and his trainer then started off again and it was another ten minutes or so before I heard any more English spoken... which was John asking me if I had got all I needed.

Whenever I ring John there seems to be organised chaos in the background with the big man invariably fielding at least one other telephone call at the same time. But he always finds a few minutes for a friendly chat and is full of sound advice.

One of the first times I ever phoned him was for the newspaper to ask for a programme for one of his forthcoming dinner shows.

"No problem," said John.

He asked where to send it.

I gave him the address and asked him to mark it 'Boxing Correspondent.'

The next day the letter arrived addressed: 'Market Boxing Correspondent...'

Every letter I have had from John since then has been addressed the same. I have never got round to telling him – not that I think he would take offence. You cannot be a boxing promoter without having a fairly thick skin.

At all the dinner shows he stages with Terry Fawthrop at the Bradford Hilton, John always smiles through, regardless of any digs directed at him by the MC. The one he suffers most is: "Guests might be interested to know John's opened a food factory and he's had a soup named after him – it's called Thick Vegetable."

John, though, is an astute and clever businessman and if it offers any consolation I was at one of his dinner shows when the same MC introduced me to the guests, saying: "I hope you can see him at the back."

He tapped the microphone and added: "You should be able to, he's a fat bastard." Well, as they say, there is no such thing as a free lunch – or a free dinner, come to that.

Even Joe Delaney had to suffer at that particular show.

The MC, warming to his task, sharpened his barbs further and said: "Now Joe, as I'm sure many of you will be aware, runs a pleasant hostelry in what I'm led to believe is a quiet little village nestling on the outskirts of Leeds.

"Harehills, I believe it's called."

A few deep guffaws from the well-heeled clientele filled the room.

"You'll know you're there because the wheelie bins are jacked up on bricks.

"Someone tried to firebomb Joe's bar last night, I'm told. They threw in a Molotov cocktail but one of the customers drank it before it hit the floor."

It did not go unnoticed by myself that the dinner-table guest boxers, including Derek, all more or less escaped the MC's scathing wit. The now late and lamented Leeds United legend John Charles got off lightly too.

Sitting next to the 'Gentle Giant', he poured me a glass of wine.

"Red or white?" he asked.

"Er, red, please."

He nodded approvingly, saying that was a good choice – red wine was good for the heart, he added. He had learned that during his playing days in Italy with Juventus.

Now that is the kind of training schedule to be encouraged.

John also spoke of his playing days at Leeds back in the '50s – and there is no doubting it was a less pampered age for soccer's superstars. Big John had to catch the bus to get to training.

He recalled the day the club chairman had pulled up at the bus stop in his Rolls Royce and offered John not a lift but a bit of sound advice – "never be late for training," he said. Off he then drove, leaving John in the drizzle to wait a little longer for a bus.

That Bradford dinner show was the same venue where Derek had made his professional debut on September 26 1994.

His opponent then had been Doncaster-born Michael Alexander, listed as a middleweight and a year older than Derek. Alexander had joined the paid ranks in January the previous year and had won seven of his 11 fights.

Derek remembers his six-round debut with mixed emotions. It was a six-twos (six two-minute rounds) though Derek said that even at that early stage he would have preferred to have been contesting a six-threes (six three-minute rounds).

"I was the most nervous I've been for any of my fights since then," he added.

Derek's dad had travelled over from Ireland to witness his son's debut. Derek also had at least 120 supporters from Delaney's all paying the £45 price for the dinner show.

"I felt a bit under pressure. On reflection it might have been easier to have started with a fight outside West Yorkshire. But there you go. I was up for it, of course, but I'd no real idea what to expect."

He had been sparring with local middleweight Marvin O'Brien.

"I think I did too much training for it. I never stopped and was coming home at night completely done in. But it was all new to me and I'd no idea if we were doing things right or not.

"The fight itself was a bit of a shock. I'd never been hit so much in my life. It was hurting a lot. I don't think I had any defence and I hadn't even known he was a southpaw. In the end I just had to dig deep. I was determined I wasn't going to lose my first fight. My heart got me through and in the end I stopped him."

The stoppage came in the last round as Derek unleashed a volley of blows and the referee stepped in to call a halt.

"I was just relieved to get that first one out of the way. But it felt good to have won. It did. It felt very good."

I asked Derek if he had had any doubts about carrying on in the game after such a hard start.

"No, of course I didn't. With that one out of the way I was just itching for the next one. The thing is I didn't feel I was getting any further and I was knackered again when I had my second fight."

That came a little over two months later and was again a six-twos in Bradford.

Seamus Casey was the opponent and he was at least a stone-and-a-half heavier than Derek.

"I was never in any danger of getting hurt with Seamus. He just kept holding on and it went the distance. It was a learning thing."

But Derek felt he was not learning enough and went to see John Celebanski, who suggested he could join trainer Kevin Spratt who had come back into the fight game after an admirable career as a pro which saw him take a Central Area title.

"My split with Ricky wasn't anything personal, just one of those things," says Derek.

As things turned out there was to be a spat with Ricky later in Derek's career arising from a fight bill and promotional material for one of Ricky's boxing shows.

Derek had objected to his name being billed for a show which he was not appearing in and Joe Delaney, as Derek's sponsor, also took exception to Ricky's use of Derek's name when promoting Leeds rival Lee Murtagh,

Lee, as already mentioned, had beaten Derek as an amateur when Derek made his debut for Burmantofts.

Joe, with the eye of a showman, issued a £100,000 challenge to Ricky and inevitably it attracted the attention of the press. To this extent the publicity put both sides in the spotlight and if you believe the old adage that there is no such thing as bad publicity, then everyone came out on top.

By this time – late 1999 – Derek was already British champion.

Joe told the papers: "Derek's name and his loss to Lee is constantly mentioned in posters and media reports based on Rick Manners' promotions. This is totally unfair."

He continued: "We want to put the record straight and I am prepared to back Derek to the tune of £100,000 to beat Lee in a winner-take-all contest.

"Derek is a welterweight and Lee is heavier at light-middleweight but I am convinced that my man would win."

He added: "It is unprofessional to constantly knock Derek who has a Lonsdale Belt to his credit and relinquished the IBO Inter-Continental light-middleweight title to box and win the British title."

Not surprisingly the press was lapping up all this. And Joe, of course, was smart enough to know they would.

Ricky responded: "I have never shown disrespect to Derek and admire him for what he has accomplished. The fact remains that Lee Murtagh has a victory over him as an amateur and we can't turn the clock back and change that result.

"Why doesn't Mr Delaney put his £100,000 into a promotion with Derek and Lee topping the bill and both boxers earning appearance money? Such a bout would settle the arguments once and for all."

The feud festered until the following week when Ricky came back again.

"I've been in touch with Lee and he is prepared to box Derek. Lee is confident he can beat him. But he insists he will not fight for peanuts. The money has to be good."

Joe countered: "I'm not a promoter. I simply want to back my man for £100,000 and it is evident that Manners is unable to match my wager. The hope is that Manners will now refrain from repeating in promotional publicity that Murtagh once outpointed Roche in his amateur days. We are heartily sick of this tiresome and unjustifiable repetition. If you look at Murtagh's professional record he hasn't earned the right to meet Roche and to sell him on a points win in his amateur days is truly scraping the barrel."

Ricky had not finished, though. "The fact that Lee beat Derek is obviously bugging him and Mr Delaney," he said.

Joe replied: "My last word to Rick is: Match my bet or there's nowt doing."

Meanwhile amid this war of words a bemused Derek was quietly preparing with coach Kevin Spratt for a British title defence.

Chapter Nine

Leeds' boxing background

OLD fight bills and yellowing press cuttings provide a roll of honour to boxers of the past.

Sadly, most of those who could remember the early warriors first hand have now either grown old themselves or passed away.

But piece together the evidence and the memories that survive and a picture emerges that reflects the social history of those days. And it is difficult to escape the conclusion that they were hard, hard times. They were also days when boxing was at the forefront of the sporting scene and the fight game provided at least a glimmer of hope to many youngsters.

"I'm 78 years of age and when I started if you weren't a boxer there was something wrong with you and everybody loved it," said fairground promoter Mickey Kiely in Vanessa Toulmin's 1999 book *A Fair Fight.*

In today's more pampered, more affluent society there are far easier options and many alternatives to a life in the ring.

But there are still men who choose to pull on the gloves and that in itself is evidence that today's fighters are still a special breed.

Boxers themselves, though, perhaps give such arguments little thought.

"Boxing's what I do," is the most likely response.

It is men such as Derek who elect to continue a legacy passed on from earlier days.

Whether or not they know exactly why they do it is perhaps another matter.

In Leeds, Derek has succeeded a tradition dating back to before the beginning of the last century.

Leeds may live in the boxing shadow of some nearby cities, like Manchester and even Sheffield, for example, which have produced a glut of champions in recent years, but Leeds still boasts a rich history of boxing.

As early as 1892 boxing shows were staged at a stable in Briggate, one of the main streets in the city centre. By 1900 there were regular shows at the Leeds County Athletic club in Harrison Street and in 1903 the Jewish Athletic Club in Sheepscar Street began to host events.

Other popular venues to emerge in the following years included Dobby Mills at Kirkstall, the Tommy Oates' gym in Holbeck and Bakers in St Luke's Street.

Joe Fox was the first Leeds boxer to win a British title, clinching the bantamweight crown in November 1915. He went on to add the British featherweight title in 1921 before retiring from the ring in 1926.

Another Leeds bantamweight champion of those early days was George 'Kid' Nicholson who took the European crown in 1928.

Then there was Johnny Britton, born in 1906, whose record between 1923 and 1933 was 175 contests, including 134 wins and eight draws. Among his notable opponents were Johnny Cuthbert in 1923, Jack 'Kid' Berg in 1925 and Harry Corbett in 1926 in an eliminator for the British title.

The number of contests fought by some of the old timers is enough to make the pugilistic historian punch-drunk with disbelief. For example Jim Oldfield, another Leeds-based featherweight, had more than 300 paid starts. He once fought a 12-rounder in Sunderland on a Saturday night, rested on the Sunday, had a 15-rounder on the Monday and was back down the pit for the night shift in Doncaster on the Wednesday.

Undoubtedly the best known Leeds boxer of that era, though, was Harry Mason, who still holds the unique distinction of having won two British titles twice (lightweight 1923-24 and 1925-28; welterweight 1925-26 and 1934).

Harry was actually born in London in 1903 but moved to Leeds as a youngster, his interest in boxing beginning as a member of the Jewish Lads Brigade. His last ring appearance, after 18 years was in 1937 when he lost to Ted 'Kid' Berg.

Leeds' reputation as a boxing city had been underlined in 1920. That was the year when the city's Town Hall hosted its first-ever boxing promotion. Perhaps not surprisingly there is no-one around now I know of who can still remember the event. I have vague recollections of my own grandfather, who boxed back in those days, telling me about it. Mind you, he used to tell me about the days when Buffalo Bill rode through Leeds on horses and Indian braves camped along Kirkstall Road – one of the major routes into Leeds – in their tepees. But then again, as local historians can confirm, it is a fact that Buffalo Bill did indeed once set up camp in Leeds, bringing his wild west show to the city.

The boxing promotion of 1920 was billed the 'Grand Assault at Arms' and included perhaps the finest array of boxing legends ever to assemble under one roof in Europe. They included Tommy Burns, world heavyweight title opponent of Jack Johnson; French legend Georges Carpentier, who won world titles at middleweight, light-heavy and heavyweight; British heavyweight champion Joe Beckett; world flyweight king Jimmy Wilde; world title challenger Frank Moody; and European middleweight champion Johnny Basham. There are still a few hard-backed programmes around that verify the claims.

Clearly, that Leeds Town Hall event was a grand affair, but the city's main venue in the 1920s was the rather more modest National Sporting Club in Templar Street.

By the 1930s the number of venues had grown and Leeds boasted fighters such as Sonny Lee, Billy McHugh, Seaman Jim Lawlor, Alf Thornhill, Benny Thackray, Little Minor, Jimmy Hayes, Joe Lowther, Johnny Durkin and Jimmy Learoyd, all now sadly gone.

Seaman Jim Lawlor was a particularly colourful character. He learned the fight trade after joining the navy as a 15-year-old and still in his teens became welterweight champion of the Mediterranean fleet. He eventually rose to be ranked eighth in the world at his weight and by the time he retired in 1939 had won 72 of his 107 professional bouts, including 10 first-round knock-outs. As well as his prowess between the ropes, Jim was something of a poet and once sent one of his verses to that other pugilistic poet Muhammad Ali, which Ali then hung in trainer Angelo Dundee's Florida gym.

Another character from that golden era was Fred 'Tubber' Burrell. He was the youngest of a family of five boxers. It was his father, a boxing trainer, who chose the ring name 'Tubber' after a boxer he knew who was killed on the Somme in World War I. 'Tubber' became one of Yorkshire's top ten lightweights despite boxing landing him in trouble with the law at an early age – he was only ten years old when he had his first paid fight.

You can imagine that might be frowned on, but it was not so much his age that caused all the bother rather the fact he stepped into the ring after 8.00pm. Apparently it was illegal for a ten-year-old to be still up and scrapping at that time of night. Happily for 'Tubber' the case was dismissed and he walked free to fight another day.

Johnny Durkin was another lightweight. His debut was on a Sunday afternoon. His next fight, a scheduled 10-rounder came soon after – that evening, as it happens.

Johnny went on to top the bills at many venues, commanding purses of £50, which in those days was a fair old sum.

One of the most famous fighters to ever appear in Leeds in the 30s was world flyweight champion Benny Lynch from Glasgow's Gorbals. His opponent was Yorkshireman Len Hampston whom he beat in the seventh round.

World War II then curtailed the careers of many boxers and marked the end of what had been a golden era of boxing, not just in Leeds, but throughout the country.

Post-war, many small halls were forced to close when the government of the time introduced a crippling tax on entertainment.

The instinct of the boxer continued, though, with men like Jackie Wakelam among a new generation of fighters.

Welterweight Jackie had joined the Army in 1941 (giving a false age) and served with the Cameronians in Singapore and China. In 1945 he became a pro boxer taking part in several promotions in the Far East, principally at a Disney-sounding venue, Happy World stadium in Singapore.

He returned to England in 1947, training at the Halfway House in the Rothwell area of Leeds.

Researching his history, the most startling moment in his career appears to have been the time he complained of a pain in his leg following one particular fight and an X-ray revealed a bullet still lodged there from a wound picked up in Burma.

Many more boxers came and went but it was not until the 1970s that the city boasted another British champion. Allan Richardson was born in the West Riding pit village of Fitzwilliam, the same birthplace of England and Yorkshire cricket legend Geoffrey Boycott.

A graduate of St Patrick's ABC in Leeds, it was in 1977 that Allan won the featherweight title, beating Vernon Sollas, from Edinburgh. Allan had turned pro in 1971 after winning a bronze medal at the Commonwealth Games in Edinburgh. His boxing career was full of brave battles, including a 15-round epic defence of his British title against Welshman Les Pickett in front of a partisan Welsh crowd. And I have been told by many English ex-pros that fighting the Welsh boys was always tough.

"Why's that?"

"Cos they're all as hard as bloody nails, that's why."

Another of Allan's epic battles was his bid for the vacant Commonwealth and British Empire titles when he went 12 rounds with unbeaten Eddie Nduku at the Nigerian National Stadium in Lagos.

A year before Allan won the British featherweight crown, another Yorkshireman, who was to become famous across the world, had won the heavyweight title.

Richard Dunn is an amiable bear of a man – the type of character who all too easily attracts good-hearted ribbing. One manager on being told of a boxing show being planned at Bradford's Richard Dunn Leisure Centre (named after the big man) replied: "Is it still standing?"

The boxer himself had a self-deprecating sense of humour

and is quoted as having said he was put down so often he had a "cauliflower arse."

But in truth, Dunn was an able boxer who had his good and bad days in the ring but found fame and fortune towards the twilight of his career, grabbing his chance of glory with both fists when it came along.

Although more often associated with neighbouring Bradford, Dunn was, in fact, born in Leeds in 1945 and raised in the suburb of Bramley in the west of the city. He was already nearly 20 when he started in boxing, having built up a bit of a reputation as a useful player on the rugby league pitch.

Richard made rapid progress in the ring as an amateur, reaching the semis of the national ABAs three years on the trot. Selected for the England team, he knocked out Irish heavyweight and future British champion Danny McAlinden on his international debut.

You might think he would have been set up for a rosy career in the vests, but boxers are often the last to know what is going on behind the scenes; what strings are being pulled. Richard was later overlooked for a place in the England squad against Scotland and, disillusioned, made the decision to join the paid ranks. That was in 1969.

He put together a tidy record over the next few years but there were disappointments as well as victories. Notable wins included the defeat of Bunny Johnson ranked fourth in Britain in 1971. But Johnson exacted his revenge in 1975 when they fought a final eliminator for the vacant British title. Dunn was put down in the fifth and seventh rounds but came back and sent Johnson to the canvas in the eighth, raising hopes that he was on the road towards becoming the first Yorkshireman since Bruce Woodcock to win the British heavyweight crown. It was not to be that year, though. Johnson clinched victory in the tenth with Dunn counted out.

Dunn's career looked to be on the edge of a downward spiral and more stoppage defeats followed before he met Neville Meade (who was to take the British title in 1981). Dunn stopped Meade in five rounds.

From then on Dunn came under the wing of veteran George Biddles who had helped guide Wally Swift and Jack Bodell as well as Hogan 'Kid' Bassey to titles. Biddles secured for Dunn a title eliminator against Rocky Campbell, a man who had beaten him in just one round four years earlier.

But this time it was Dunn's turn to taste glory and the ref stopped the contest in the seventh.

Now aged 31, Dunn was to fight for the British title for the first time.

It was 1975, his seventh year as a pro and his 39th fight. His opponent was once again Bunny Johnson and in a 15-round battle he won decisively on points.

Dunn's beaming face became a popular and familiar sight on local television and in the papers as he prepared for his first defence only 35 days after securing the title. Defeat, though, would have marked his reign as champion as the shortest in boxing history. His challenger was outright favourite Danny McAlinden but Dunn upset predictions by beating the Irishman in just four minutes.

Next came the European crown with victory over surprise contender German Bernd August for the title that had been left vacant by Joe Bugner.

And then came the ultimate challenge, his memorable showdown with The Greatest, Muhammad Ali in Munich on May 24, 1976.

Most people will know the outcome. Life is not usually penned by the same people who write the fairytales and in the fight Ali quickly adapted to Dunn's southpaw stance. After a string of knock-downs the battling Yorkshireman was counted out on his feet.

One footnote of that fight is that it was to be Ali's last KO in the ring.

A tale concerning Richard Dunn that sticks in my own mind came from a sportswriter who had the unenviable task of interviewing the boxer in the changing room after his stoppage by Bugner. No boxing hack relishes such jobs but it is something of a code of honour, (which might surprise those of you who doubt there's any of that quality in journalism).

Anyhow, the writer was allowed access to the changing room and as his story goes he was standing in the sombre atmosphere, trying to wear a sympathetic smile and offered Dunn a pat on the shoulder.

Dunn looked up.

"So what are we doing?" asked Richard, clearly still groggy. "Are we ready?"

There was a moment of hesitation as the writer assessed the comment.

"Er, it's all over Dickie," he replied, eventually.

"What?" Dunn paused. "What is?"

"The fight. It's finished."

"Eh. What happened then?"

The writer looked around suddenly realising he was faced with informing Dunn of the result. No one else was at hand.

"Er, you lost."

"What?"

"You were knocked out, Richard. Sorry."

There was a moment of disbelief on the boxer's face.

"Aw no," he moaned. "Aw no."

He was getting visibly distraught. "I've let everyone down. Aw no."

At this point the trainer arrived and decided the best course of action was to help Richard face the facts. He did this with a sharp slap across the face. It did not have quite the desired effect, though. For the second time that night Dunn was sparked out.

For Dunn, that Bugner defeat was more or less the end of his career. He fought again, this time in South Africa, but lost to Kallie Knoetze.

The possibility of an outright Lonsdale belt, with the British title vacant once again, was not enough to lure Richard back to the ring and it was doubtless a wise decision when he announced his retirement. He was a far wealthier man than he could have imagined only two years earlier. He had also been awarded the status of hero in his home city and county.

Soon after Dunn's decision to retire, Leeds' Tom Collins was about to emerge on to the professional scene.

The former Market District amateur made his paid debut in 1977. He went on to take the British light heavyweight title three times, twice became European champion and challenged for a world title.

Caracoa-born Tom's first title, however, came in 1980 when he beat Greg Evans inside the first round to take the Central Area title in Bradford.

Managed by Trevor Callighan, he first took the British crown in 1982 against the celebrated Dennis Andries and defended against Trevor Cattouse (at the Astoria in Leeds) and Antonio Harris. Tom was to lose his title to Andries and then lost a rematch. He then won only two of his next seven fights. But in his second Leeds appearance – at the Town Hall in 1986 –Tom was back in the frame with victory over Winston Burnett.

He regained the British title with a win over John Moody. In his 11th year as a pro, Tom became European champion, beating Dutchman Alex Blanchard with a round two KO. He vacated the British title. It was another Dutchman who was to take the European title off Tom – Pedro Van Raamsdank. But the Leeds man was to regain the British title for the third time when he beat Tony Wilson in Reading.

After failing in his bid for the WBC title against Aussie Jeff Harding in Brisbane, Tom reaffirmed himself by beating Frenchman Eric Nicoletta to regain the European crown. He defeated another Frenchman, Christophe Giraud, a few days before Christmas 1990 but it was to be Tom's last victory. He was given another tilt at a world title – the WBO – which was the first such bout to be staged at the Leeds Town Hall. American Leonzer Barber, however, took the vacant crown when Tom, suffering a huge swelling on his forehead, was not allowed out of the corner by Trevor Callighan for the seventh round. Anyone who saw that swelling, by the way, would realise the word "huge" was no overstatement – any bigger and there would have been Town Hall officials asking about planning permission.

Tom went on to lose his European belt to German Graciano Rocchigiani and confirmation that it was all over for the big man came when he was demolished by Johnny Nelson in Mansfield in the first round of a bid for the Sheffield fighter's WBF cruiserweight title. Another notable landmark in Tom's career was that in 1989 his fight with Mark Kaylor was judged to be the Best British Contest of the Year by the Board of Control.

Collins' career spans an era that brings us up to the time when Derek Roche had begun to fight as a pro.

As well as Derek, there have been other notable Leeds fighters, but two in particular who stand out are Henry Wharton and Crawford Ashley.

Leeds-born Henry, another fighter whose amateur career was spent at the St Pat's club, where he was nurtured first by Harry Hare and Terry O'Neill, reached the ABA finals in 1989 before turning pro. He lifted the Commonwealth super middleweight title in only his 11th paid start, beating Aussie Rod Carr in a thrilling clash at Leeds Town Hall.

The British title came five fights later, Henry having successfully defended the Commonwealth against Lou Gent, Nicky Walker, Kenny Schaefer and then a re-match with Carr.

He took the British crown at Elland Road in a dual title fight against Sheffield's Slugger O'Toole aka Fidel Castro Smith.

Henry's three pro defeats were all world title challenges – all 12 round epics. The first was against Nigel Benn for the WBC super middleweight in February 1994. It was after this fight that Henry split from trainer Terry O'Neill, who had guided him since the amateur days and co-managed him with Mickey Duff. Terry was also to take Derek to his WBU world title challenge at Bethnal Green in London.

At the end of 1994, Henry, by now trained by Gary Atkin, got a second chance at a world crown – this time against Chris Eubank for the WBO version of the title. He tried again in May 1997 but again lost on points, this time against Robin Reid.

Henry was to fight only twice more after that – both bouts in 1998 and both victories.

Henry famously announced his retirement, much to the

shock of Gary Atkin, only days before a scheduled clash with Crawford Ashley in 1999.

His record though stands proud – 31 contests, 27 wins, three defeats and a draw. It is an opinion shared by many that had Henry managed to win any of his world title bids he could have shifted into celebrity status outside the boxing world possessing as he did charm, good looks and eloquence.

His reason for retirement was simple: he had done all he could, he said.

He told me: "I'd put everything I had into boxing, squeezed out every last drop of energy, every inch, every ounce and I'd nothing left to give. Nothing. I went as far as I could and that was it."

It is hard not to be moved by the passion of his argument, the recognition that he had pushed his mind and body to limits few people would even dream of.

One man less than impressed, however, is Crawford Ashley who still smarts from the cancellation of his showdown with his fellow Leeds fighter.

Yet Crawford, who announced his retirement in 2002, a few months short of his 38th birthday, can look back on his own great career with pride.

Twice he won British and European light heavyweight crowns plus a Commonwealth title and twice he challenged for major world titles in America.

Crawford started as an amateur at Montagu Burtons and then Rocky's when Burtons closed. He then competed for Burmantofts ABC which had grown out of Rocky's.

He had about 60 amateur bouts, twice winning schoolboy finals and twice clinching Junior ABA titles. His brother Glenn, four years Crawford's senior, won the Senior ABA light-heavy title in 1982. Crawford signed for Halifax's Tommy Miller in 1987, beating Steve Ward on his debut. It was the first of 29 stoppages he inflicted on opponents in his 44 paid-fight career.

Many of his fights are particularly admirable as so many were contested in "the lion's den" – time and time again he fought opponents in front of hostile, partisan crowds.

His first title came in 1989 when he stopped Manchester's Carl Thompson for the vacant Central Area light heavyweight belt. Crawford's next fight after Thompson is one that sticks in his mind – he stopped former England amateur captain Brian Schumacher in the third round at Preston.

In March 1991 he made his first bid for the European crown, losing a split decision to Graciano Rocchigiani in Germany. In October 1992 he tried again, this time drawing in Italy with Italian-based African Yawe Davis. There was never a re-match.

It was in March 1997 that Crawford finally lifted the title, demolishing Spanish champion Roberto Dominguez with a third round KO in Liverpool. In the meantime though Crawford had won the British title – twice – having relinquished it once and had also earned himself that treasured Lonsdale belt outright.

He first picked up the British crown defeating Roy Skeldon in July 1991. He defended against Jim Peters – knocking him out in 55 seconds – and then Glazz Campbell.

In 1993 came his famous challenge for the WBA super middleweight title against one of the finest pound-for-pound fighters in the world – America's Michael Nunn who had lost just one of his 40 bouts. Crawford, managed at the time by Barnie Eastwood, took the fight at three weeks' notice. And so it was once more into the lion's den, this time in Memphis.

In November 1994 Crawford beat Cardiff's Nicky Piper in a ferocious battle in the Welshman's home city to regain the British title in what was widely regarded as the best British bout of that year.

Crawford, oddly for a victor, offered him a return, but Piper, nowadays a TV boxing pundit, went on to challenge WBO champion Dariusz Michalczewski.

There was another world title challenge for Ashley though – this being in April '95 for the WBA light-heavyweight title while he was with Frank Warren. Again it was in the USA, this time against Virgil Hill.

Back this side of the Atlantic, though, and after beating

Dominguez for the European belt, Crawford defended against previously unbeaten French champion Pascal Warusfel in Paris, winning on points. But then came the shock defeat against Norway's Ole Klemetsen at Muswell Hill in October 1997. What went wrong against the "Golden Viking"?

Crawford simply says: "In boxing you're always just one punch away from glory and one punch away from disaster."

Just three months later, back from sparring with Lennox Lewis in Big Bear, California, Crawford was once more fighting for the now vacant European title, this time in York against previously undefeated Frenchman Jo Siluvangi. Both Crawford and Henry Wharton won that night, Henry stopping Ukrainian Konstantin Okhrey.

All looked set for a Yorkshire money-spinning showdown between the two Leeds-born men. Sensationally, though, three weeks before the fight scheduled for February 6, 1999, 31-year-old Henry announced he was quitting the ring.

That bombshell, though, was not the first such disappointment to hit Crawford's career – in 1996 three-times WBC champion Mike McCallum had pulled out of their scheduled bout with only days to go.

And there was worse to come.

After losing his titles to Sheffield's Clinton Woods, Crawford was due to fight boxing legend Thomas 'Hitman' Hearns in Detroit in March 2000. Crawford, though, was told on the final day of his training programme in Tenerife, that the fight, for the IBO world cruiserweight title, was off.

But Crawford is a philosophical man – he says that his only big regret is that he fought only once in his home-city.

Latterly, Crawford and his wife Hayley have opened a box-ing gym and leisure complex in Dewsbury, just down the road from Leeds, with Crawford having secured his professional coaching licence.

Chapter Ten

Delaney's and working the door

NEW YORK has its Hell's Kitchen, so why not call the Chapeltown/Harehills area of Leeds 'Purgatory's Pantry.' Or how about 'Lucifer's Loft Extension'?

But good people trying to make life better for everyone in the city's less privileged communities deserve more than cheap shots.

Even so, Harehills ain't Beverley Hills.

Countless numbers of cars pass through daily, travelling to and from the city centre. Yet for many commuters it is not somewhere they stop.

As they sit at traffic-lights, immune from the outside world, they may stare at the multi-ethnic street-life outside the cut-price stores and take-away shops.

They may even look up and see the ragged Irish tricolour flying from the domed top of Delaney's Bar on Roundhay Road or notice the awnings that hood the first-floor windows.

It is unlikely, though, that many will have ever dropped in for a quiet pint or chat.

But for those in the know, Delaney's is a haven.

It boasts a roguish charm. And for the Irish it is a reminder of the old country.

First-time visitors, it has to be said, might have initial problems finding the entrance, which is down a side-street, equidistant between the bins of a supermarket's rear yard and a workshop with a sign that says the company pressure-cleans lavatories.

But do not be put off.

I am no architect, but I would say the entrance door is flanked by small pillars perched on which is a Roman-style pediment adorned with a couple of shamrocks and the name "Delaney's Bar" in a Gaelic typeface.

To reach the bar you have to climb a steep flight of carpeted staircase that leads to a thick wooden door with a sturdy peep-hatch, which Derek, or whoever is on duty, can slide back and decide if you are welcome or not.

Earlier on in the evening or during the day you can usually walk straight in.

When you are familiar with a place it is sometimes hard to think back to your initial impressions.

My only advice is that when you visit, worry not.

The recently refurbished interior – décor selected by Derek's partner Tracei no less – has a welcoming atmosphere and even when the place is quiet you would never say the place lacks character.

Memorabilia abounds to please the most demanding of Hibernian stalwarts, though this is no manufactured Irish-theme pub.

The pictures of old Irish heroes, including a framed cutting of Derek, are a statement rather than merely decoration.

And the seasoned shillelagh that hangs behind the bar looks capable of being more than just an ornament.

You certainly do not have to be Irish to be welcome at Delaney's but it perhaps goes without saying that you would be unlikely to win any best-dressed customer award wearing a bowler hat or, let's say, a Glasgow Rangers shirt.

I once joined a group of older men at a table and they were talking about someone who had been shot by a British soldier, allegedly in the back, while lying on the ground. The conversation grew increasingly agitated but I was puzzled as I had not heard anything of the incident on the news.

I asked when it had happened.

"That would have been in 1916," replied one of the group.

But in my own experience the banter of the bar is nearly always good humoured and you are unlikely to leave the place without some tale to remember the place by.

You may see men marching round the pool tables with cues over their shoulders like rifles as rebel songs play on the juke box; you could have conversations with old men and probably hardly understand a single word; and there will be times when the place is so packed that the main floor will be just a sea of people.

On one such busy occasion, I remember, a spot of trouble broke out and the whole floor seemed to sway from side to side like an undulating tide.

At the time, I was talking with both Joe and Derek at a table on a floor slightly raised above the teeming mass of bodies.

Derek could spot where the trouble was coming from and said: "I'll be back in a minute."

He then turned and swallow-dived into the melee disappearing and re-emerging moments later at the source of the aggravation.

Joe looked at me and apologised.

"I'd better give a hand. 'Scuse me just a moment."

He then stood up and dived in himself.

True to their word, they were both back at the table soon after, order once more restored. The conversation resumed as if nothing had happened.

Sometimes, though, matters can be a little more serious.

Derek recalls an incident that began after he ejected two men from the premises.

By this time Veljko, Derek's Serbian friend who had been with him in Bournemouth, had moved to Leeds and was working alongside him at Delaney's.

The following evening the two men who had been ejected by Derek were back but this time armed with clubs and knives and with a few more pals just for good measure.

"There was a quite a few of them," says Derek. "And it all kicked off but we got them back out through the door.

"Then they started to try to smash their way back in. It was all a bit chaotic, with fists and pool cues flying. The place was going mad. Anyhow, and I don't know where it came from, but suddenly I notice someone has hold of one of them CS gas cylinders or grenades or whatever it is you call them. I don't know if you've ever seen this stuff but one squirt of it at one end of a big room and your eyes will be burning even if you're standing at the other end. It's powerful stuff. So it's a bit of a shock, you might say, when the next thing I know is the whole cylinder has gone off. There's this gas everywhere. It's blowing all around the club. People are climbing out of the windows and on to the sills just to get away from the gas. I think there was about 20 people out on the little window ledge above the street. There's people screaming, crying and pouring down the stairs, blinded by the gas. Jeez, what a scene, I'm telling you... Everyone had to get out and they're falling about all over the place. There was ambulances and police all turning up too. It was like a riot scene, that you might see on television. People crying in the street from the gas, they were."

Derek stops his tale abruptly and shrugs.

"You know, there's not trouble like this all the time," he says. "It's one of the things about being on the doors – 99 per cent of the time you're just hanging around and having a chat now and then with the customers. But you've always to be ready for that one per cent when something kicks off. You've got to stay alert all the time and that's what's the tiring thing about the job.

"And sometimes I do get mad with Joe. The other week, for example, I'd had to ask this fella to leave."

There were several factors about the man's appearance and manner that might have rung alarm bells in Derek's mind. The man moved in a way suggestive of someone who expected people to get out of his way; his face, while boasting no obvious scars, folded with aggressive lines down his gaunt face and his eyes burned with drunken anger. What Derek liked least about him, however, was the six-inch kitchen knife he waved in Derek's face.

"He was wanting to cut me up. Well, I'm not too happy about that as you might imagine, so I deal with him. But the thing is that the next day I walks into the club and there's this same fella again and he's there having a chat with Joe at the bar.

"So, I says to your man 'Listen, I've barred you just last night' and then it's Joe who says 'Aw come on Derek, your man's all right, he was just having a bit of fun.'

"We don't always see eye to eye on everything, Joe and me, that's all I'm saying."

Derek then mentions another spot of bother, as if as an afterthought.

"There was the time these 30 or so bikers wanted to come into the bar – you know Hell's Angel type bikers, not the kind that pedal up the Yorkshire Dales on a Sunday afternoon. Anyhow I had to say: 'Not tonight, I'm sorry lads.'

"Well, they weren't over the moon about this, as you might imagine. Veljko's by my side which is nice because in situations like that you need a diplomat."

Veljko diplomatically broke two pool cues in half, one thick end for himself and one thick end for Derek.

"The thing is," says Derek, "you've got to stand up and be counted. We had to let them know they weren't welcome in Delaney's or they were going to smash the place apart. Anyhow, we battered them down the stairs and I'll tell you what, we let them know we'd be none too pleased to see them back again either."

So no bikers' reunion at Delaney's then?

"No, I doubt that," smiles Derek. "But to be honest I get sick of it all. I've put my neck on the line too many times. People have tried to knife me, bottle me, glass me. So far I've not been shot at. But there are times when you've had enough."

An incident I recall, which did not involve Derek, occurred one early midweek evening when the club was less than busy.

A few ageing regulars with care-worn faces sat in silence along the far wall, nursing pints in shovel-sized hands.

Several people, including an elderly couple, stood at the bar talking and laughing while two youths amused themselves playing pool.

I sipped at a glass of Guinness while Joe drank coffee from a large mug.

We were at the far side of the room discussing an article for the newspaper. As is Joe's way we were at a table rather than at the bar, which is Joe's way of indicating that what he has to say is important.

The conversation started with pleasantries before we approached the point.

It was just being reached when a thin hand nervously rested on the table.

Joe looked up.

An ageing man in a suit and open-necked, checked shirt stood in front of us nodding a little nervously.

"Joe, " said the old man softly.

"Not now Sean, I'm having a business conference," said Joe.

The man hesitated and backed away a little.

"I was just after wondering, Joe," he continued.

"Go away Sean, it's a conference here we're having, can't you see?"

But the old man persisted.

"I was thinking would it be 'right to be taking some of your beer mats?"

Joe's expression didn't change.

"Just a few, you know," added the old man, hopefully. "It's only a few I'm after."

"Is it a pub or what you're setting up, Sean? I'll talk with you later."

The old man turned and began to shuffle away, a slight sway in his walk. He stopped and turned back.

"It is not for a pub, Joe."

"Is it not?"

The old man forced a smile. "No. It's for Mary, the wife, Joe."

"It's Mary's collecting beer mats now, is it?"

"No, not that Joe, it's just Mary's fallen down the stairs and I'm needing some mats to soak up all the blood."

Doubtless, readers will be relieved to know that Mary was not badly hurt.

Chapter Eleven

Climbing the rankings

KEVIN SPRATT has the kind of face that looks like it has been walloped hard with a heavy-bottomed frying pan... and then walloped again just for good measure.

But it is a face with a lot of character. It has a pugnacious charm that I daresay impresses clients both inside and outside the boxing game. And, to be sure, Kevin's built himself an admirable reputation as a promoter in recent years.

An ex-Meanwood amateur, Kevin happily ignored advice not to turn pro and went on to build up a very decent record, clinching the Central Area welterweight title along the way.

After hanging up his gloves, Kevin returned to boxing when John Celebanski gave him the chance to be a trainer.

Derek joined his camp soon after, following his split with first trainer Ricky Manners.

Another interesting note about Kevin is that he has a cousin also called Kevin Spratt. It hardly beats George Foreman, who has five sons all called George, but it is a good start nonetheless.

The Roche-Spratt double act was to go far.

As Derek mentioned in an earlier chapter, the understanding between a boxer and his trainer is vital. Both Derek and Kevin hit it off from the start and Kevin's 'in-your-face' thoughts on fighting were well suited to Derek's forward, aggressive style.

Derek had not long to wait to put his training to the test with his first fight under Kevin coming just seven weeks after that victory over Seamus Casey.

Again fighting in Bradford, Derek made it three wins in three, stopping Carl Smith in the third.

"Smith was big and muscular but didn't cause me many problems," said Derek. "I finished it with a combination."

Next up came Charlie Paine in Hull. It was another stoppage, this time in the first round. Paine was counted out.

There was another first-round stoppage on that same show, Sheffield's Clinton Woods dispatching Paul Clarkson. It was Woods' third paid start on the road to glory which ultimately led to his challenge against the man regarded by many as being the world's best pound-for-pound fighter, Roy Jones Junior, for the American's world light-heavyweight titles.

Derek was back in action only four weeks after the contest in Hull, this time in Rothwell on the south east edge of Leeds. It was March 1995 and it was to be Derek's first and only appearance in his adopted city for another seven years. It was a points win this time, over six three-minute rounds against Rob Stevenson.

"I had him down in the first round, I remember," said Derek. "He beat the count but I went in to finish it off and he caught me and down I went."

It was the first time in his six-month professional career that Derek had been put on the canvas.

"It was a little bit of a shock being put down for the first time, nothing serious, though, and you learn from it. I got back up and finished the job."

Derek was to suffer a more serious knock down while British champion, however.

His aggressor this time was smaller, lighter and put him in hospital.

"But it was an accident," chips in Tracei.

The couple had been in Bridlington on the Yorkshire coast on a day out and, ignoring all the resort's countless bounty of attractions, had been kicking a ball around. About to depart, Derek was putting the ball back in the boot of the car just at the moment Tracei decided to slam it shut.

You can probably guess the rest.

The boot crashed down on Derek's head knocking him senseless.

"I was out for a while, just lying on the grass. When I eventually opened my eyes I could see all this blood on the grass. It was a funny sensation and I remember being sort of mesmerised watching the blood soak into the ground as it pumped out of my head. Then I saw Tracei looking scared.

"When I saw her face, I couldn't stop laughing."

And Derek is laughing again as he recalls the incident.

"I had to go to hospital and they glued my head back together. They didn't use stitches."

The consequence of the accident, apart obviously from me making a mental note never to play football with Tracei, was that Derek failed his next brain scan.

Scans are compulsory for all pro boxers and, apart from being expensive, are conducted annually. They have to be passed for a fighter to retain his licence. Fortunately for Derek a second opinion gave him the all clear.

Derek's next two fights after the Rothwell match were also six-round points victories.

"Paul King was the first of those two and he was a good boxer," recalls Derek. "He was Northern Area champion at the time so I was pleased to win that one. Hughie Davey was next and that was a real war. We just stood toe to toe for the whole six rounds and slugged it out."

Derek had now been a professional for 12 months and had won all his seven fights. There were to be two more, though, before the year was out.

He boxed Rick North on November 11 1995 – Armistice Day. But there was no peace for North as Derek demolished him over the first two rounds before the referee stepped in to wave it off.

"That was another pleasing win because North was one of Brendan Ingle's men and Brendan was in the corner for the fight."

The Sheffield trainer was at that time entering a golden era with Prince Naseem, Naz having won the WBO world featherweight title against Steve Robinson just six weeks earlier. The Ingle-Naseem partnership was sadly to turn sour later.

"Yeah, I was pleased to beat North," says Derek.

With just two weeks to go before Christmas, Derek entered the competitive ring once more.

"That was against Kevin McKenzie. The first two rounds were the toughest I'd ever had up to that point. I was hitting him with all I'd got but I didn't think I was hurting him. That can be disheartening for a boxer. But you just have to keep going. Then we banged heads and my nose got smashed. It was the first time I'd had my nose broken properly. I'd had it bust and bleeding a few times before, obviously, but this was the first time it had been really mashed up properly. And it hurt."

Derek knew that he was going to have to dig deep, show raw courage and pull out something special if he was to avoid this fight becoming his first defeat.

"Like I said, I thought I hadn't been hurting him but I must have been because I just kept up the pressure, kept banging away and he folded in the third round. And I tell you what, I was glad to finish it and get my nose seen to."

So Christmas came with Derek still boasting a 100 per cent record and there was the added bonus that any local panto wanting to fill the role of Rudolf the Red Nosed Reindeer had a ready-made option.

By the way, should ever you be tempted to crack such a joke to someone who has broken their nose it is perhaps best to check their suffering has eased. People in pain can be a mite touchy. For example, a pal of mine by the name of Steady Dave once had his nose smashed playing golf for the first time when he stood behind his brother who was driving off and no one told him about the club's back swing. It was a long time before he could smile when people asked if he was still feeling a little below par.

Of course, you can break your nose in a lot of sports – not usually playing golf, mind you. But in boxing it is not so much an occupational hazard as a near certainty.

Referees, though, are unlikely to stop a professional boxing bout because of such an injury, unless blood is flooding back into the fighter's mouth and he is swallowing the stuff.

It says a lot about boxing that fighters so often battle on despite such damage.

Pain or no pain, Derek was back in action again within two weeks of the New Year. It was over to Halifax where his opponent was again Seamus Casey and once more it ended in a points victory over six rounds for Derek.

"I remember I took that one at very short notice," says Derek, who with that win had reached double figures in his pro career without defeat.

He made it 11 out of 11 in the first week of March 1996 when he stopped Wayne Shepherd in the third round. It was his sixth stoppage and the Roche-Spratt double act was building up a decent reputation.

There was a sixth-month gap though before Derek next fought again.

"I'd been in hospital for two weeks with a mystery virus," said Derek. "I never knew what it was but I'd wake up in the night and I'd be dripping with sweat. The bed sheets were just soaked through. I'd stagger to the bathroom with a high temperature and a blinding headache. But I'd no idea what was wrong. Obviously I wasn't training, I was just too ill. I went down to under 10 stone for a while which was the lowest I'd been since a kid. I just felt really, really weak."

But once out of hospital, it was to be only 10 weeks before his next contest: a challenge for the Central Area welterweight belt. The fight was his first scheduled 10-rounder and his first opportunity to clinch a title.

"To be honest I wasn't back to fitness when we took the fight but I wasn't going to let the chance go by."

His opponent was Scunthorpe's Trevor Meikle who had won the title in his home town seven months earlier against Kevin Toomey.

One advantage for Derek was that back in his fighting days Kevin Spratt had twice met Meikle, with honours shared – one victory apiece. So Meikle's style was well known within the Roche camp.

The fight went ahead on September 23.

"I knew I wasn't 100 per cent for it but like I say I wasn't going to give up the chance of a title. I still felt I'd beat him. In the end it went the full ten rounds but I won every one of them and I had him down in the sixth or seventh too.

"It was nice to win a belt, for sure, but I saw the win as a stepping stone. I had my sights set higher."

Boxers, though, have to be patient. Bursting with ambition, Derek kept busy and four weeks after Meikle, he faced south east based Paul Miles whose last fight had been in France.

If boxers have to be patient between fights sometimes they have to be even more so at the venue itself.

Derek was supposed to box at 8.00pm on the bill against Miles but was then told the fight had been put back to nine. There was no reason given but then he was told it was being cancelled and soon after that it was back on again.

"I'd been hanging around for hours before we actually boxed," says Derek.

Waiting around to box does little to calm the nerves.

"It's unsettling because you warm up, ready to box and then have to stop and you get cold. Then you have to warm up again. No boxer likes it."

It should not be forgotten that fight nights are the culmination of weeks, possibly months, of training for the professional boxer and it is little wonder that the few hours or so leading up to the bout are a testing time, more so when the stakes are high. Any delays, then, can be unsettling.

But then again most boxers have been in the game since they were young and have their own ways of coping.

An almost ritualistic atmosphere prevails in the changing room as the trainer carefully tapes a fighter's hands ready for battle. In the opponent's room the same 'ceremony' is being performed.

And every individual has his own way of preparing for the looming conflict.

Derek, for example, admits that he always wears the same socks for each fight.

"One of them things, it is. You can't explain. At one time I used to always have a bottle of the Holy Water with me but I gave that to a friend of mine who was dying with cancer."

At one dinner show, I was in the changing room with the fighters before the bouts and one of Derek's stablemates, already gloved up, was turning, as best he could, the pages of the *Boxing Yearbook*.

If he was anxious he did not show it – and it was only his second fight.

First of all he looked up details of his opponent. There was no picture of the man, which was a disappointment and so he continued looking up other fighters in the book, interjecting with comments like: "Jeez, will you look at the face on this fella? You'd not want to fight him on a dark night" or "what about this one – at least he'll never be having to worry about losing his good looks."

It all helped to lighten the mood.

At amateur shows the atmosphere is also often intense before a bout, particularly as the time between the weigh-in and the contest can be hours. Again, though, there are always some lads whose nonchalance is amusing, if not startling.

I was once sitting with a group from the Meanwood club in Leeds. The boxers were watching the action in the ring while waiting for their call. I turned to give an encouraging nod to the lad, aged about 12, who was on next, and he offered me a crisp from the packet he was munching. What was spectacularly impressive was that he was wearing his gloves but still managing to force the crisps into his face and past the gum-shield he was already wearing.

Needless to say, by the end of the first round the lad was looking more than a mite queasy. Fair dues, mind you, he took defeat well and, after picking up a trophy for competing, still managed to finish his crisps.

Another incident that raises a smile was at another amateur show when I was talking to a trainer while the boxers were killing time waiting for the show to start. Someone's mobile rang, filling the room with the theme tune from the *Rocky* film. About six lads all reacted, each one reaching for his mobile phone.

Derek's fight against Miles finally went ahead hours after it had been scheduled.

Perhaps after all that waiting around Derek was sleepy, because he got caught in the first round by Miles.

"I was on my arse with a left hook near the end of the round. I got up, though, and when the bell went I went back to the corner. John Celebanski was in my corner and he rushed into the ring at the bell and told me to sit down so he could see I was OK.

" 'I would if there was a stool to sit on,' I shouted. He'd left the stool outside the ring. I couldn't stop myself laughing."

Perhaps the incident cheered Derek up because he went into the next round and flattened Miles with a big right hand over the top.

"And that was that," adds Derek.

Gary Beardsley was his next victim.

"He was a nice boxer but just wasn't strong enough and I caught him clean," Derek recalls.

That was another second round stoppage and his last fight of 1996.

Derek's first fight of 1997 came in the February and was against Doncaster's Michael Alexander.

Recalling that encounter still seems to make him angry. "He just kept whacking me in the balls. I was beating him up in that fight and would have finished it. But he must have hit me low about four times. OK you can get hit in the balls now and then but this was just blatant and Mickey Vann, who was refereeing, disqualified him.

"I was mad at it being stopped. I told Mickey so afterwards and said that I'd wanted to stop him myself. Mickey said he'd just been doing his job. He said shots like that could have ruined my career... and a lot more besides. And he was right, of course."

Derek was by now moving quickly up the ladder and four months later was to face his stiffest test yet. He was to defend his area title but more importantly the contest was an eliminator for the British welterweight belt.

His opponent was Brendan Ingle-trained Chris Saunders who had already worn the British crown before losing it to Beckenham's Kevin Leushing.

Leushing himself had gone on to win the IBO world welterweight title, beating Cirilo Nino in New York and then challenged for the IBF belt against American great Felix Trinidad in Nashville, Tennessee.

Saunders, though, had beaten Leushing in a previous encounter, stopping him in the fourth round at Ebbw Vale.

"I was nervous for this one," admits Derek. "Saunders had been British champ and was a hero of mine. I really admired him. But I trained hard for it and was the fittest I'd ever been when I climbed into that ring.

"I knew this was a big one. It was the first time I'd met Tommy Gilmour who had come down to see me box."

Glasgow fight boss Tommy, of course, was to become Derek's co-manager alongside John Celebanski.

"I wanted to impress," says Derek.

And impress he did.

"I just beat Chris up. No two ways about it. I beat him up. I remember he came at me and threw a right uppercut but I cracked him with a great left hook and connected first and knocked him down.

"I also remember that he slipped later on and fell through the ropes. My dad was there pushing him back into the ring. He should've been holding him down."

Eventually, the referee had seen more than enough and stopped the contest in round four.

"It was definitely my best win up to that point," adds Derek.

Derek, however, suffered an injury in that fight that has burdened him ever since. During a clinch, his left arm was bent back at the elbow.

"It's not a problem most of the time, but sometimes I get hit on one particular spot and the pain is agony. It lasts for about 10 or 15 seconds and then goes away. If I'm sparring and it happens I just turn away. Obviously I can't do that in a proper fight. I've never found out what the problem is exactly. Maybe it's a splinter of bone or something. When I saw a doctor about it he asked me to measure the pain on a scale of one to ten. Well, I'm in the hurt game but I can tell you the pain is about nine on the scale. One day I'm going to have to try and get it sorted out. But it might have to wait until I retire. We'll see."

Chapter Twelve

Courage and carrying on

FEAR is a part of human nature and is something everyone has experienced at some level or another. Boxers are no exception.

The idea of climbing into a ring to face someone intent on rearranging your features obviously qualifies boxing as a scary pursuit.

But Derek says: "My one fear before a fight is losing. After all the hard work that you go through and for all the people in your life, you don't want to lose. That's obvious, isn't it? I want to do well. It's not a fear about being hurt."

Perhaps that is a predictable reaction from a successful pro boxer. Paid fighters, or for that matter anyone else involved in dangerous sports, tend not to dwell for too long, if at all, on the possibility of injury.

But fear, or more accurately the conquest of fear, is an essential element in the fight game and one, it might be argued, that goes a long way to justifying boxing as a legitimate sport.

Now if that sounds complicated, paradoxical or, worse still, dull – apologies – readers can skip this chapter if they want – but be warned: there is no refund on the cover price.

For boxers, fear is an emotion they have to learn to control. To do otherwise is to invite defeat.

It is commonly acknowledged that some boxers are beaten before they even climb into the ring, intimidated into submission. And who can blame them?

Fighters like Mike Tyson are famous for having thrived on the fear factor they impose on opponents. It is easy enough to believe – one of the tabloid newspapers once estimated the survival time of a normal man in the ring with Iron Mike would be less than two seconds. And they were talking death

113

not KO. Where they plucked their figures from, who knows? But it sounds plausible enough.

Sonny Liston was another boxer who thrived on menace. His wins over Floyd Patterson, for example, were probably such convincing victories because Patterson seemed to have lost the self-belief that he could emerge victorious.

The psychological battle can be won before a punch is even thrown. Experts in verbal warfare designed to unsettle the opposition have been plentiful – Nigel Benn springs to mind: "I get worried when a guy goes down, in case he doesn't get up – for me to hit him again."

And not all fighters can find it in their hearts to be magnanimous in victory, thus enhancing their fiercesome reputation for the next bout with a few well chosen words. Take Jerry Quarry after he had beaten Britain's Jack Bodell: "They told me Jack Bodell was awkward and he was... he fell awkwardly."

But fear and courage are bedmates. The bravery of boxers is in overcoming fear – the will to battle on – and that is one of the most highly regarded of human qualities.

It is, perhaps, why some boxers talk of their fights as being a battle within themselves as much as against an opponent. They are slugging it out with inner demons.

To develop this argument, perhaps it is not a bad idea to compare boxing with other spectator sports. Take football. Apart from being 'the beautiful game,' football's attractions involve pageantry and tribalism. Fans ally themselves to a soccer team with a passion, adorning themselves in club colours and in worryingly extreme cases living their lives according to the fortunes, or misfortunes, of their side.

Boxing tends to be exciting on a different level, but where the two sports differ in particular, is that, aside from worry about defeat, football lacks any real fear factor. Football is a physical sport, but rarely an overtly dangerous one, (unless you want to include the Leeds and Chelsea matches of the 1970s).

Boxing on the other hand is, undoubtedly, a dangerous

game. And overcoming the fear factor is an integral part of it.

There are numerous other dangerous sports around, of course, and one of the great attractions to participants is the peril.

As Derek has said, it is the fear of losing, not of being hurt that concerns him.

The first part of this statement relates to an anxiety shared by all sportsmen. No one wants to lose. But for professional boxers, other than the journeyman, the consequence to his career of defeat is usually much graver than it is for a footballer. In some instances a single loss can be enough to stall a boxer's career. A series of defeats can wreck it.

The second part of Derek's statement also needs consideration.

Derek says he does not fear being hurt.

That does not mean to say he fails to recognise the danger. The courage of boxers is in the conquest of fear. In other words boxers control the fear or anxiety that comes from being aware of the dangers and use it to their benefit in the ring. Senses are heightened; reactions sharpened; strength is exaggerated. Fear no longer impairs the boxer's performance; its hidden presence enhances it.

American legend Oscar De La Hoya summed it up when he said: "I learned long ago to live with fear – controlled fear. Anxiety, panic or outright fright, that's fear out of control. Being relaxed, anticipating punches, translates into fear under control."

This conquest of fear is an experience shared by participants of other dangerous sports.

In reality, some of those other sports are more dangerous than boxing; statistics show there are a far greater number of serious injuries and fatalities in rock climbing, car racing, motorcycling and horse riding, for instance. And there are a far greater number of serious injuries in, say, rugby.

Yet there are few people who seem to clamour to see those particular pursuits banned.

But one argument from the anti-boxing lobby is that when

people are injured in other sports it is an accident, whereas boxing is the only sport where it is the intention to hurt an opponent. Put another way it means that in most other dangerous sports participants are competing against the elements as opposed to boxers who battle against another human being.

This might seem a valid point, but it is a moral rather than a medical argument – at the end of the day an injury is still an injury whatever the intention.

So, what is the moral defence for boxing?

Maybe it can be argued that it starts with the fact that, unlike most other dangerous sports, boxing is a spectator sport and for it to be so it is obvious that it demands competition between opponents.

To that end it means that boxers perform not just for their own satisfaction but for a crowd. Now, that in itself might seem objectionable to some people, but it has to be tempered by the fact that boxers are participating because they want to do so, in other words they are consciously choosing to box.

As Derek says: "No one forces you to be a boxer. You do it because you want to."

The majority of fans watch it for many of the same reasons the boxer chooses to pursue it. The fans witness a triumph of courage over fear as well as celebrate the hard-earned skills of the boxer. Remember, too, that in the licensed game very few men who should not box manage to slip through the net. Medicals are strict, and, even in border line cases, there are few trainers who would be prepared to take on a fighter they thought was at risk even if somehow that fighter was to be granted a licence.

In its intensity, the sport allows an audience a glimpse of the experience the boxer is going through. Of course, it is not the crowd in there taking the risks, yet an empathy with the fighter does exist. It puts the fan in touch with that element of human nature that he or she might otherwise rarely experience in normal life. It provides an insight into survival and that conquest of fear.

Another, more light-hearted argument might be that the ritual of the sport also actually provides a safety valve against violence. It allows a certain type of fan to indulge their macho tendencies by dressing up as if for some 'Hard Bastard' fashion parade without actually having to prove they really are a 'Hard Bastard.'

Naturally a lot of gold jewellery helps the image and some fans clamp on so much of the stuff it is a wonder they can still stand up under the weight.

Back to the main argument, though.

Boxing is not violence for violence sake. And it is not violence fuelled by anger inside the ring. As Derek says: "An angry boxer is a loser."

Of course, sometimes trouble does kick off outside the ring, just as trouble can flare at football matches among certain types of people when emotions are running high.

By chance, I am writing this the day after witnessing a spot of bother at a dinner show, though for me it is the circumstances rather than the scrap itself that are memorable.

Guest of honour at the show was former world champion Chris Eubank, a great fighter and seemingly a nice bloke too. I approached him and for some inexplicable reason greeted him with: "Hello, Chrith."

Happily, he took no offence. At least he did not knock my head off. Dubliner Steve Collins, a man who, of course, beat Eubank, was once asked if he had liked Eubank and had replied: "Course I did, he paid for my house."

Anyhow, Derek was sitting next to Eubank and with no fight looming Derek had been giving the complimentary red wine a bit of a hammering. By the second fight on the bill he had fallen asleep, his head resting on the table as industrial quantities of alcohol weaved their magic on his grey matter. Fellow boxing guests James Hare and Dale Robinson, meanwhile, kept turning their heads and wore nervous smiles, not unlike schoolboys who expect the headmaster to walk in at any moment. Dale tapped Derek's shaven head every so often to try to wake him up.

Then trouble erupted near ringside when a fan rushed forward, followed by several more from the same table. The security men moved quickly and for a minute or more there were 20 or so powerfully-built men swapping shoves, punches and heavy-browed scowls.

What was surreal about the incident, though, was that an unruffled Chris Eubank carried on signing autographs and Derek... well, he began snoring.

Of course, there are always going to be some fans who get over excited. The same happens at a lot of different sporting events. By and large, though, most boxing fans behave themselves. And very few go to a show in the hope of seeing a boxer get hurt. Those that do might be advised to seek medical help. Most can appreciate why it is that a referee steps in to stop a fight. They have sympathy as well as empathy with the boxer. There is humanity in the sport.

What is also important to recognise is that at least at licensed boxing shows security is tight. There are also many safety measures in force, including medical staff, inspectors, proper match-making etc, to ensure the minimum risk possible to the boxers themselves.

It is not being alarmist to say, and it has been stated many times by people with more standing than myself, that if boxing in this country was banned it would go 'underground' and a lot of the safeguards would, therefore, disappear. Many other professionals would simply box in other countries – Ireland or America for example.

So for those pragmatic reasons alone, apart from the more honourable reasons outlined, boxing would seem to deserve its place on the sporting calendar, distasteful as it might appear to some people.

There are times, perhaps, when boxing does itself few favours such as when promoters go into overdrive, encouraging fighters to spout pre-bout nonsense and stage-manage bust-ups for the TV cameras. But the boxers and most fight fans recognise this for the ploy it is. So I am sure do most other people.

Sometimes real animosity does exist between two fighters, which is a little disturbing, but watch boxers after a fight and more often than not what you see is mutual respect.

Win or lose, having had the courage to climb into the ring is a victory in itself.

But doubtless, despite all these arguments, many in the anti-boxing camp will remain unconvinced and though it is only right to respect the views of those who do not like boxing, those who accuse it of being "legalised thuggery" are being unfair.

It calls to mind a story of Derek's relating to a time when he was being treated in hospital after a fight.

He was suffering a bad cut above an eye which needed stitches. Having had so many stitches over the years he forgets which particular fight this incident followed.

The hospital doctor, who clearly had little sympathy for boxers, told Derek he considered boxing a barbaric sport.

Bearing in mind that this was after the fight and the natural pain-killing adrenaline in Derek's body had ebbed, the doctor then proceeded to sew up Derek's wound without anaesthetic. Worse, though, was that he was, to put it mildly, heavy-handed with the needle, pulling and tugging hard and making comments like: "You won't be bothered by this, will you? You're a boxer, you're a hard man, aren't you?"

Derek said: "He thought I was just an animal. Because I was a boxer, he thought I had no feelings. I felt like screaming but just took the pain. I wasn't going to give the bastard the satisfaction."

It hardly needs anyone to point out who the thug was in this instance.

It would be unjust to suggest that that particular doctor was typical of the anti-boxing lobby. The majority of people opposed to the sport are motivated by what they see as the best of reasons.

There is one question I have been asked on occasions, which deserves an answer, and that is how would I feel if someone close to me was seriously injured or worse still, because of boxing?

The answer is simple: I would be devastated.

I have known people to be hurt in boxing. I have also known people killed mountain climbing, smokers who have died from lung cancer; drinkers whose livers have been destroyed; people who have lost limbs motorcycling. I have also known people who have led blameless but dull, long lives.

The fact remains that people have a choice in life and boxing is a choice.

There are occasions when, personally, doubts or ambivalence do creep in, usually when one witnesses a fight that is not stopped as early as it should be because either the corner fails to throw in the towel or the referee delays calling a halt. It is rare for this to happen, though, and it should be said extremely rare in Britain where standards are high. When it does occur, it is an error of judgement and is ugly and inevitably harms the sport's reputation.

There are also some fighters I would prefer to see quit the sport simply because it is too hard on them or their families. Yet they find it hard to walk away. The lure of the gym can be very strong.

For many, boxing provides the one platform where they can truly express their own identity – a place where they can demonstrate their natural abilities.

My own sympathies are with the boxers, which is why I feel they should be under no pressure from promoters, managers or anyone with financial interests to take a fight they do not want or if they feel less than 100 per cent on the night.

But Derek thinks differently. "If you're a boxer, that's what you do," he says. "You go out and get on with the job."

It is an admirable sentiment but I guess I am made of weaker stuff.

I remember a retired professional telling me how it was always "we this and we that" before a fight and then he laughed and added: "but they used to get out of the ring when the bell rang."

But the truth is that most boxers I know love the sport and very few professionals do it solely for the money.

Ultimately, it comes down to the fact that people should not be expected to live their lives wrapped in cotton wool. So many critics of boxing, I suspect, have little idea of the mentality of the fighters themselves. Boxers are generally fighters in life. They are often men with big hearts, big dreams and a lust for living with all the dangers that go with that. Most come from a background where the thought of being compelled to lead someone else's idea of a safe but sterile existence is incomprehensible.

And, to be honest, most do not give a crap what any of the anti-boxing lobby think, anyhow.

In some ways boxing is a reflection of the blunt end of life, with pain and tragedy ever willing to intrude.

One man who might be expected to know this better than most is Yorkshireman Paul Ingle who was IBF featherweight champion and a former undefeated British, Commonwealth and European champion.

In December 2000 he was battered into a coma defending his world title against South African Mbulelo Botile in Sheffield.

Paul then entered his toughest ever fight – a battle for life.

Thankfully, he survived but there's no getting away from the fact he suffered a degree of brain damage.

But Paul has maintained that he has no regrets about his life as a boxer despite the injuries and he still speaks fondly of the sport that brought him fame, respect and wealth and he still follows it.

"On one night, I was unlucky," he has said.

One of the recommendations that followed Paul's tragedy was a closer monitoring of training to diminish the risk of dehydration.

All efforts to make the sport as safe as possible without killing its essence are to be applauded – the brain scans, the proper timing of weigh-ins, improved medical care in the corners, the reduction in rounds and the raft of other measures brought in over recent years.

Many of the bad practices some people still associate with boxing, because they still see them in old movies, are now consigned to history. That is not to say that the risks have all been eliminated and it is not to say that there is still not room for improvements.

I would even support the introduction of headguards into the professional ring if they were proved to constitute an effective safety measure.

Derek, though, is very unimpressed by such a notion.

"Why not?" I ask, looking at his shaved head "It wouldn't ruin your hairstyle much?"

Derek just about manages a smile.

He says: "Headguards are all right for sparring, I'm OK about that, but not in the real ring. When you're slipping punches..." Derek moves his head from side to side to demonstrate "...you're talking about an inch or so. Your opponent's not missing you by a couple of feet or nothing. Wear a headguard and all you're doing is giving him a bigger target.

"Also he's more likely to catch you and if you've got a headguard on it could spin your head and you could end up with more damage.

"When you get inside, too," Derek continues, "there's always the chance the other bloke will use his arms to pull the headguard down below your eyes. You're blind then and an easy target."

"You mean, he cheats?" I ask.

Derek casts me a withering look.

"You're not getting into that ring to have a picnic, you know," he says. "They call it the hurt game for a good reason. Anyhow, besides all that, headguards are uncomfortable and hot."

One safety aspect that Derek concedes he would like to see introduced concerns rehydration. He fails to understand why the controlling authorities ban any fluid other than water in the corner.

"These new isotonic drinks are absorbed by the body quicker than just plain water and if you were allowed to drink them between rounds it would help prevent dehydration. The board's recognised that dehydration is something that leaves a boxer more vulnerable to injury so I do not know why they do not just change the rules.

"There's no banned substances in the drinks and if both corners used the stuff then there'd be no advantage to either side. It's just a matter of safety, I'd say."

The controlling authorities, however, are a conservative bunch when it comes to such matters. To some extent their caution is understandable as it is their duty to ensure fair play in all contests. Thus there is a whole rack of regulations governing everything from 1-1000-adrenaline mixes for cuts to a ban even on sugar in water during a fight. Derek tells me that before one fight he had been using a nasal spray to relieve a blocked nose and was told by the officiating doctor that he was lucky to have been using that one particular brand as there was another on the market which might have led to his disqualification.

No one, of course, would condone the use of drugs to gain a potentially dangerous advantage but Derek's point about isotonic drinks does seem, at the very least, worthy of consideration. It should be remembered too that a boxer can drink as much of the stuff as he wants before or after a competition.

In an interview with *Boxing News* magazine, Simon Block, the General Secretary of the British Board of Control, made some interesting points.

He said: "It's crucial that we keep abreast of medical developments and ensure our procedures are always under review so we can tighten the plugholes or introduce new measures where there are gaps or deficiencies."

Another point is that the British Board of Control is not a statutory body but governs solely by the consent of its licence holders. It does, though, have a high "duty of care" placed on it by the courts. As a consequence, as Mr Block says: "The Board has very sophisticated mechanisms in place as to how a boxer gets their licence in the first place, who he gets in the ring with, how that contest is judged and what happens if a boxer suffers an injury as a result of that contest."

Oddly, there are some people who are not particular fans of boxing, or possibly even dislike the sport, who nevertheless see nothing wrong with celebrity punch-ups, or what has become known as white-collar boxing.

Here is a quote from the *Radio Times* magazine of October 1 2003: *"It wouldn't surprise me if this splendid programme about white-collar boxers spawned regular live coverage on a cable sports channel. Watching middle-class professionals pummelling each other mercilessly for two minutes at a time is much more fun than most world title fights."*

Well, obviously, witnessing a couple of overpaid lawyers knocking seven shades out of each other has a certain appeal but in reality the risks of allowing two under-trained, unskilled men into the ring is potentially more dangerous than any professional bout. Yet people, most of them probably not boxing fans, would be prepared to watch it on TV, ignorant of all the risks and possibly seeing it as nothing more than a bit of a lark.

Little wonder, then, the board of control has washed its hands of all such bouts.

They know what the risks are and are committed to minimising them.

At the end of the day, though, boxing, is never going to be risk free.

One boxer who comes to mind is Leeds' Jimmy Lowther, who was a stablemate of Derek's.

A 5ft 11in light-middleweight, he fought as Gypsy James Lowther and was a strong but elusive fighter whose record before his last fight was a creditable 13 wins in 16 outings. He also had an admirable amateur record with Hunslet Boys' Club in Leeds and had boxed for England in the vests.

His ring career was to end after a 12-round tilt for the IBF Inter-Continental title against gifted Mehrdud Takaloo at Bethnal Green, which he lost on points.

The events that followed might almost be comical if not so serious.

Travelling back from London as one of manager Keith

Walker's passengers, Jimmy began to complain about his head and that he was feeling sick.

Keith decided to take no risks and reckoned the best thing to do was find a hospital. Not surprisingly in a strange town neither he nor any of his passengers had any idea where the nearest one was. It was then that Keith spotted a parked-up police car and pulled up behind it to seek help.

The officer, looking in his rear view mirror, was alarmed to see a Mercedes late at night behind him full of large men. He then saw someone climbing out of the car and approach him.

Presumably, fearing for his own safety, the policeman slammed his car into gear, put his foot down and sped off.

Keith then raced after him and a chase followed with the Mercedes in hot pursuit of the cop car.

It was only when Keith managed to speed up close enough to the police vehicle, flashing his lights, that he was finally able to persuade the officer to stop and secure an escort to an hospital.

Ultimately, Keith's actions more than likely saved Jimmy's life as the boxer was taken to surgery to remove a clot on the brain.

In spite of all this, only a few weeks later Jimmy was keen to pick up his career again. There was no question of him getting his licence back, though. Somehow convincing Jimmy that his fighting days were over was a hard task for those concerned.

As was said at the very beginning of this book, sometimes boxers refuse to acknowledge when it is time to quit. That is understandable, as most of them will have been involved in the sport since an early age. It is what they know. To suddenly expect them to put all that behind them is asking an awful lot.

Derek, himself, contemplating his own retirement from the ring, acknowledges this.

One particularly famous example is Frank Bruno, who for 197 days was WBC heavyweight champion before retiring after defeat at the hands of Mike Tyson. Frank found retirement from the ring hard to bear. At the age of 42 – seven years after his defeat but still one of Britain's best-loved sport stars – he was sectioned into a psychiatric hospital after suffering depression.

Former world champion Barry McGuigan, appearing on a television news programme to talk about Bruno's condition, spoke of the vacuum felt by many fighters when their boxing days ended. He pointed out how a boxer's life was almost monastic in its routine and discipline and when that then ended there was all too often a sense of hopelessness for those who had not prepared themselves properly for the break.

As is often the case, the media had been quick to jump to conclusions, with some pundits blaming the physical punishment of Frank's career for his mental downfall. Few acknowledged that they themselves might in any way have contributed to Frank's condition.

Thus, when news of Frank's misfortune was published, *The Sun* newspaper's front page splash headline read: 'Bonkers Bruno locked up.' After a deluge of angry complaints the newspaper replaced the headline in later editions with: 'Sad Bruno in mental home.'

Marjorie Wallace, the chief executive of the mental health charity Sane, described the initial coverage as "ignorant."

The fact remains that in Britain anyone in the media spotlight seems to be fair game for criticism in his or her private as well as public life. Boxers, despite their exterior toughness, are no better prepared to cope with such insults than anyone else, possibly less so.

And in Britain anyone who enjoys success seems to become a target to be knocked down.

Take for example what Robert Philip wrote about Frank Bruno in the *Daily Telegraph* in 1995: "If Frank Bruno insists on calling himself a world champion, then he is a champion only of the portion of the globe not inhabited by any number of superior heavyweights including Ridick Bowe, Mike Tyson, Evander Holyfield, Lennox Lewis, Bruce Seldon, George Foreman, Luciano Pavarotti, Keith Chegwin, Mr Eric Younghusband, 22 Bramble Lane, Stoke Poges..."

Amusing in a smug sort of way, perhaps – though you might wonder when it was that Mr Philip last got into the ring with Mike Tyson.

It should be remembered boxers have feelings too and it might be wondered what cumulative effect constant barbs have on anyone's mental stability. It sometimes seems that open season is declared on some individuals when it is perceived as acceptable for anyone to jump on the insult bandwagon and have a go, regardless of whether or not they have any idea what they are talking about.

Big Frank Bruno may have had some weaknesses as a fighter, but so what? Ultimately, his achievements are those of a boxing hero.

Fans might recall that he had wanted to return to the ring, aged 42, for at least one more chance of glory against Audley Harrison. Despite sympathising with Frank's desire to recapture the old days, it was widely recognised as being one quest too far.

It is often pointed out that of those boxers who have suffered serious damage it seems a significant number have done so because they have insisted on carrying on past their fight-by-date.

It is those at the very top who are the most likely to continue for too long. In some instances they are lured along by the thought of just one more big pay-day but more likely it is the opportunity to feel the excitement of youth once more that is so irresistible. Those who stick with the professional game solely for the money are fewer in number than might be imagined – for most of them there are easier ways to earn a crust nowadays.

Possibly the most worrying aspect of all this, though, is the thought of any boxer being coaxed into continuing in the game too long by others all too eager to extend their own meal tickets.

But there is a danger, also, of being patronising; boxers are individuals and as such have as much right to make decisions as anyone else.

As heavyweight Evander Holyfield told *The Guardian* newspaper in September 2003: "People want to decide my life for me. They keep reminding me that I'm turning 41 next month. They keep telling me boxing's a brutal business. Man! Do they think I don't know that? I been in the ring three times with [Riddick] Bowe. Twice with Lennox Lewis. I beat Larry Holmes and George Foreman. I whupped Mike Tyson twice. I had my ear chewed off and spat on the ground in front of me. I've seen everything it is possible to see in boxing. I know this business better than anyone. So I live and die by my own decision."

Another quote from Holyfield is: "It thrills me to struggle sometimes. That's life – it's not easy."

As it happens, Holyfield was to lose his next fight to James Toney in Las Vegas. No one could question Holyfield's courage and determination but it was evident his reflexes were no longer what they once had been.

Chapter Thirteen

Locked up in Scotland

AN early-morning wake-up call is rarely welcome. Less so when it is the police doing the waking-up.

Derek opened his front door to find two officers wanting to ask a few questions.

They told him it was in relation to an alleged traffic offence in Scotland.

"But I've never been to Scotland," said Derek.

The officers were hardly impressed. Adopting that language peculiar to Her Majesty's constabularies, they suggested that Derek might like to accompany them to the station.

And off he went, though, he did not exactly like to.

"It was a fact that I'd never been up to Scotland," says Derek. "I was a bit puzzled, like, but they said it was about a traffic offence so I wasn't all that worried."

At the Killingbeck station in east Leeds, Derek was put in a cell and having been at work the previous night he took the chance to take a nap.

"I slept OK and was nicely rested when they came to let me out. I was thinking that they were letting me go and that everything had all been sorted out. I was thinking I might as well run home when suddenly they put me in this cop car. I wondered if they wanted to give me a lift back. They didn't. They drove me all the way up to Scotland instead.

"It's a long drive, I'm telling you that.

"I ended up in Kirkcudbright, I think it's called, but I still didn't really know what it was all about. It was a Friday and that was bad news for me because they told me I was going to have to appear in court...on the Monday.

"They weren't interested in one thing that I'd got to say.

"So they locked me in a cell again. And I was there all weekend.

"There was six of us in this one cell, I remember, with just mattresses on the floor and a toilet. I didn't sit on that toilet all weekend, I'll tell you. It's probably just as well because one of the fellas in the cell was a meths drinker and he was so thirsty all the time that he kept drinking from it. He'd scoop out the water with his hand and have a slurp. We kept shouting out for water but they never brought us any.

"It stunk in there as well," adds Derek. "A couple of the fellas, nice lads they were, had been caught poaching for salmon and they'd tried to escape down the river. The police had sent in the dogs to get them. I bet they gave the dogs a wash after, but these lads in the cell they were stinking of fish all weekend. Terrible smell, it was."

On the Monday they were let out of the cell one by one and allowed five minutes to wash their hands and faces under a cold tap before being locked up again.

"I was thinking to myself this is all a bit harsh for some driving offence. I wondered what they did to you in Scotland for something really serious."

Derek was soon to learn the accusation against him was failing to provide documents having been stopped for speeding.

"I couldn't work it out. I tried to explain it hadn't been me but no-one seemed interested. They just didn't want to listen. Even the solicitor they got for me in court was no better. He didn't give a bollocks. In court they just gave me bail. Then they told me to go home."

Derek manages a smile. "Well, I was wondering what happens now? I asked this copper how I was supposed to get home. He just told me that it was my fucking problem."

There was a stroke of luck for Derek, though, and one for which he is still grateful – one of the alleged poachers he had shared the cell with had left him five pounds at the station to help him get home.

"I used the cash to phone Tracei back in Leeds and she went and bought a train ticket and that was faxed up to Scotland.

"I had to get to Dumfries to catch the train and ended up

thumbing a lift. That was another story. I got picked up by this woman who said she'd just come out of prison for stabbing her husband. Great journey that was. Anyhow, she got me to Dumfries without pulling a knife out, so I was OK.

"I remember I got back to Leeds at about 1.30 on the Tuesday morning. A nice few days I'd had. I can think of better ways to see Scotland, that's for sure."

Derek's ordeal was by no means over. He discovered that the person who had committed the offence of which he had been accused was a friend – a friend he had shared a house with in Bournemouth, as well as the one who had put him up in Leeds when he had first arrived.

Derek does not want him named in this book.

"I was just disappointed. It hurts when a mate lets you down like that. He'd known all my personal details so when he got stopped by police he'd just said that he was Derek Roche."

It turned out that he had pulled the same stroke more than once. In all, Derek received 11 summonses from around the country for various traffic offences.

"If he'd come and told me what he'd been doing we might have sorted something out but he never said a word and it was me that landed in trouble. I suppose I could have told the police exactly what had happened but I'm not a grass so I kept quiet.

"I eventually got off all the charges except a couple but I had to go down to courts in places like Enfield in London and Northampton and some in Leeds.

"When I went down to London for one of them I got to court too late and the case had already been heard. I'd been fined and had some points put on my licence. I asked to see the judge or whatever he was and told him that if it had been me who was guilty then I'd have just paid the fine but I'd spent more than £200 getting to court to tell them it wasn't me.

"To be fair, he was sympathetic but said there was nothing he could do as the case had already been dealt with.

"By the end of it all I ended up with a couple of fines and a six-month driving ban.

"It ruined my friendship with your man, that's for sure. I'll still speak to him, like, if I see him but things can't ever be the same."

During this episode, Derek had been to see his ex-friend who by this time was in prison for a separate offence.

"We were supposed to have an hour's visiting time but he wouldn't come out of his cell to see me. Eventually he did come out for the last five minutes and mumbled that he'd see me all right when he got out. He never has, though. It makes me sad more than anything because I'd always thought we were such good mates."

Derek was to return to Scotland again, this time voluntarily, in February 1998. A British title challenge was looming and fights were becoming less frequent. Before that trip north of the border he first of all faced Hughie Davey in Bradford, a man he had beaten previously.

"I'd won on points that last time. This time I stopped him in the third. I was pleased with that because in all his 30 or so fights Hughie had never been stopped before."

By now signed up with Tommy Gilmour, and with top cutsman Benny King in his corner, Derek ventured to Glasgow for his next match. It was his first paid start outside Yorkshire and he boxed Darren McInulty.

"That was on Sky television, I remember. It was just a six-threes and I had him down in the fourth but I felt terrible going into that one. I was only about 60 per cent fit to be honest when I fought him and he was very awkward. I still won on points, though."

Asked why he was only 60 per cent fit at the time, Derek said the fight had come at short notice and he admitted that he had enjoyed a better Christmas than perhaps he should have done.

"I didn't have time to train up to peak fitness but I was still confident I'd come through OK. And I did, though it wasn't ideal."

There was to be one more contest before Derek challenged for the British title.

Chapter Fourteen

In the witness box

MEANWHILE, another friend of Derek's was to land him in court once more – but this time as a witness. The charges against Veljko Cerevic were more serious than alleged driving offences, however.

Veljko, aged 33 at the time, was charged with attempted murder. He had come to Leeds from Bournemouth and was working with Derek as a doorman at Delaney's Bar before the incident that landed him in court. The other charges against him were causing grievous bodily harm with intent and possessing a gun with intent to endanger life. Veljko had denied all charges.

His case came to court in October 1998.

Perhaps understandably, it is an episode Derek seems uncomfortable talking about. He was called as a witness having been one of the last people to see Veljko before the sorry tale unfolded.

The trial took nine months to come to court and followed a shooting on New Year's Eve 1997.

The jury at Bradford Crown Court was told that Veljko had been making attempts to see his 11-month-old daughter after the breakdown of his relationship with the girl's mother, Marie Stronach. The court was told Veljko had telephoned Marie asking to see his daughter but she told him he would have to see a solicitor.

It was established that Veljko had driven the 25 miles from Leeds to the home of Marie's sister Sarah and Sarah's boyfriend, police officer, Phil Little, in Silsden, near Keighley, north of Bradford. Veljko had with him a handgun – which the jury was told Veljko had thought was an imitation firearm.

Sarah, who was 21, told the court that she'd been getting ready to go out to a New Year Eve's party when her boyfriend

Phil became involved in a violent struggle on the doorstep of their home. She said she came out of the house and saw Veljko sitting astride Phil hitting him over the head.

She told the court: "I shouted 'oh my God.' Veljko turned round, aimed the gun at my chest and pulled the trigger. I screamed and ran into the house holding my left arm. I'd lost control of my arm and at one point I thought my arm had come off so I grabbed it with my right hand. I was aware that I had been shot."

She told her sister that she had been shot and Marie phoned the police.

Veljko then came into the house with Phil, the court was told.

Sarah said: "He was pointing the gun at Phil's temple. Phil was stable but covered in blood. Veljko looked scary."

She was to spend 12 days in hospital and underwent two operations.

Earlier in the trial Phil had stood up in court and said Veljko had pressed the gun against his temple. Phil said he had thought the weapon was an imitation. "He kept saying 'Phil, I'll kill you' and 'Phil, I'll shoot you.' "

Phil continued: "I told him to do it. He pulled the trigger, or I presume he pulled the trigger, because I heard a click.

"When it clicked he looked at it, holding it up in the air. He looked at me and said 'It must be your lucky day, Phil.'"

Phil said it was only later when Veljko shot Sarah that he realised the gun was real.

The court was also told that during the incident, Veljko had put the gun to his own head but it had failed to fire.

Tests had later revealed that the weapon jammed because the cartridges were too large for the chamber.

During the nine-day trial, Veljko had insisted that he thought the gun, which he had bought for £30 in a pub car park two weeks before the incident, was an imitation.

He said he was "shocked and surprised" when the gun went off. He said he had been to the house in Silsden because he wanted to see his baby. He had ended up wrestling outside the house with Phil Little and had pulled the gun from his waistband. The weapon, he said, went off as Phil tried to grab it and a bullet had hit Sarah.

Derek was called to the witness stand during the trial.

He told the jury that Veljko had asked to see him on the New Year's Eve and arrived at his home later. He had appeared very agitated and upset. He told Derek that he wanted to see the baby.

"He gave me a big hug and said if they don't let me see the child you won't see me again. I've got nothing else to live for."

Derek then said that he had tried to persuade Veljko not to go to Silsden but Veljko had ignored his pleas and driven off.

Derek added that the day after the shooting, Veljko rang him and said: "it was never meant to happen."

In the call Veljko claimed that Phil had had hold of his wrist with the gun in it and that Sarah had got on his back or grabbed him.

Questioned by the defence barrister, Derek was asked what sort of doorman Veljko was.

Derek said: "The best. He never had to use force. He was so cool."

After the incident Veljko had given himself up to police. It was Derek who had persuaded him he had to turn himself in. There had been press releases issued by police warning people not to approach Veljko but appealing for help in tracing him.

"I just told him that if he didn't hand himself in they'd eventually catch him and they'd lock him up and throw away the key."

At the end of the trial the jury cleared Veljko of attempted murder and also found him not guilty of possessing a firearm with intent to endanger life. Their deliberations then continued over the allegation of causing Sarah Stronach grievous bodily harm with intent.

The following day the judge discharged the jury after it failed to reach a verdict on the last charge.

The prosecution indicated that they wanted that charge

re-tried and Veljko was remanded in custody until the next trial which was scheduled to take place at Sheffield Crown Court. The case, though, was switched to Bradford on January 8 1999 and Veljko finally walked free when the judge decided it would be unfair for a trial to take place. The judge accepted submissions from Veljko's defence counsel, James Stewart QC, that his acquittal on the other charges arising out of the same incident meant that the case had effectively been decided already.

Mr Stewart said the grievous bodily harm charge had been added at a later stage and that a guilty verdict at that stage on that charge would be "manifestly inconsistent" with the acquittal on the firearms allegation.

Veljko had spent a year in custody awaiting trial.

Looking back on the episode, Derek has little more to say other than to add it was a sorry affair.

There were to be other shooting incidents on the fringes of Derek's life. One is dealt with only at the very end of this book.

Another involved a fellow Leeds boxer Denzil Browne.

Denzil was gunned down in a pub car park in Potternewton, near the Chapeltown area of Leeds, on May 16, 2000.

He was a victim of the tenth shooting incident in Leeds in less than two months.

Miraculously, Denzil survived despite being hit three times as 35 rounds of semi-automatic fire riddled his vehicle.

The previous day, in an unrelated incident, two men, one from Chapeltown, Leeds, the other from Manchester had been found executed in a car on Darfield Street, Harehills, not far from Derek's home.

Denzil, meanwhile, was treated under armed police protection at an undisclosed Leeds hospital.

His partner immediately spoke out to scotch rumours that Denzil was in anyway involved in gangland drug wars.

She said: "He's as shocked as me. He was just in the wrong place at the wrong time."

A couple of years after the shooting I was talking to Denzil at the pub he was running in Leeds about his plans to make a return to the boxing ring.

We spoke about his creditable boxing career, which had seen him win the Central Area cruiserweight title.

Inevitably I mentioned the shooting, too.

Denzil is a big, physically intimidating man, with fists like shovels, and I was a little wary about raising the subject but he did not flinch and simply said the incident was in the past.

Then without warning he stood up and dropped his trousers.

"This is where the bullets hit me," he added pointing to the scars. "I'm a lucky man."

And by that he meant he was lucky to not only be there to tell me he was lucky but also to be still able to tell me in his deep bass voice.

If I was a little alarmed by this the next incident moments later at least relieved the tension.

Denzil went behind the bar to fetch me a pint – he does not drink himself – and there leaning up at the corner was an old bloke wearing a face like a slapped backside.

He was rattling an empty glass in his gnarled hands irritably.

"Sorry," said Denzil not having realised the man had been waiting for a refill.

"I've been waiting ten minutes," grumbled the aged one.

"Tell you what," replied Denzil, not wishing to inflame the old man's wrath further, "have one on the house. What you having?"

The man said: "Guinness."

Minutes later, after the drink settled, Denzil placed the glass on the bar and said: "On the house for being so patient."

The old man nodded, picked up the pint, looked at it closely and after a long pause, muttered "It needs a top up, this un."

So it goes to show – just when you think you've seen it all...

I did not talk with Denzil about the shooting any further but it did strike me that it might have added to what appears to be a popular public perception that boxers so often seem to live their lives with a backdrop of violence.

Recently I went to a boxing show with a friend, another boxer, and we stopped off to pick up one of his relatives. The relative had just crawled out of bed and was stripped to the waist which gave him the chance to show me his bullet wound – it was the size of my fist. There was also a long scar leading off where surgeons had opened the flesh to extract all the shrapnel after the bullet burst inside his back.

It made me wonder about the violence that seems so prevalent nowadays.

Then, while reading up on a bit of local history, I came across the story of Leeds Irish champion Kid Saxby who had his hands injured by revolver shots as he tried to cover his face in an incident outside the Jewish Athletic Club and that had been back in the early 1900s.

So maybe violence is not such a new phenomenon as so often perceived.

Derek listens to all this patiently and then after a moment of contemplation says: "I don't think boxers are mixed up in trouble any more than anyone else, to be honest.

"OK, sometimes some idiots might want to have a pop at a boxer because they want to prove to their pals how tough they are and a boxer's not likely to be the kind of bloke who runs away. But I think it's more to do with the fact that most boxers come from tougher, poorer areas where violence is more likely to happen. It's on the streets. Like everyone else, if you're in these areas the more chance there is there'll be trouble round the corner. And if there is any trouble or whatever, people will says oh so and so who's a boxer was there – even if he's had nothing to do with it. Also a lot of boxers do the kind of jobs like door work where there's going to be bother flaring up now and again. But that's not the fault of the boxer. It's just life.

"Listen there's tragedy and sadness all over the world. Everybody's life is affected by it at some time. Boxers aren't any different, no matter what people think. Some people just think we're mixed up in violence because they see boxing as being violent.

"OK, I know that violence is a part of boxing but it's not what boxing is about. You ask me if I think about the violence when I go into the ring. The answer's no. I don't go in thinking I want to beat this bloke to death. Maybe that's what some people want to hear but it's not true. I want to win the contest, for sure. That means I've got to fight. But it's not anger I feel in there. I've said before an angry boxer is a loser. You've got to be in control of yourself. Sure I want to put the other fella down but not because I want to hurt him, it's because I want to win and if I knock him out he's not going to do the same to me. The principle's the same in any sport, you want to win and beat the opposition."

Derek grows animated as he recalls the feelings of being inside the ring.

"The concentration when you're in the ring is really, really intense. You can't afford to lose concentration. If you do then wham, that's probably it – all over. The nerves are there before the start but once you're into the fight it's concentration and the nerves disappear. You're not really aware of anything else around you. You shut it out. You've got a job to do and the other fella wants to stop you doing it.

"Once a fight is over, you're happy that the other man is OK. And you're glad you've won. It's about respect not violence."

Chapter Fifteen

Problems with publicity

NOVEMBER 6 1998 – the day after Bonfire Night and Derek had saved up his fireworks for his bid for a second title to add to his Central Area belt. It was a contest for the vacant IBO Inter-Continental light-middleweight crown.

The venue was The Hilton Hotel in London's Mayfair against Del Bryan, a former double British welterweight champion.

Both fighters had agreed on a weight-limit of 10st 10lbs.

Bryan boasted an admirable record and had boxed for the European welterweight title in 1994, losing to Jose Luis Navarro in Cordoba, Spain. In 1997 he had lost a challenge for the British light-middleweight title against Ryan Rhodes.

Bryan had taken his first British welterweight title in 1991, beating Kirkland Laing over the 12 rounds, and won the title again in 1993, this time against Pat Barrett at Bethnal Green.

With more than 50 fights to his credit, the Nottingham-born southpaw was 32 years old when he faced Derek. It would be wrong to suggest he was the force he had been but he was still regarded as being a potentially dangerous opponent.

Derek took the fight at four weeks' notice.

"It wasn't a long time to prepare for a 12-rounder and I'd been out of action for about eight months but I'd kept in shape at the gym and we just stepped everything up to get ready for the fight."

He also revealed soon after the contest that – as politicians might say – he had been "a little economical with the truth" at his pre-fight medical.

"I guess I shouldn't have taken the fight, really, because I had a trapped nerve in my back but I kept quiet about it when I was examined by the doctor."

Contests usually become less frequent for boxers as they

climb up the rankings, partly because there are fewer other fighters of the right quality around, but mostly because they have become prized, valuable assets and the price needs to be right for them to put their careers and reputations on the line. A bad loss at such a stage in a fighter's career can be devastating to his future progress.

Derek, though, as he says, was eager to get back to work and had every confidence in his ability to climb higher.

"Tommy Gilmour gave me this one as a stepping stone as well as to keep me active. I knew I had to win, mind you."

A good crowd travelled over from Ireland and down from Leeds for the London showdown.

"As you move up and the quality of opponents gets better you notice the difference, obviously," says Derek. "The biggest difference is that the better fighters are harder to put down and when you do have them down they tend to get back up again. You have to get that into your head, to realise it's not going to get easier.

"Del was a very awkward southpaw and it took me to the tenth round to wear him out. I had him down a couple of times before that, I remember."

Derek, though, is not a boxer who has ever been overly troubled by the southpaw stance.

"I was brought up with southpaws as an amateur. Back in Ireland there were about eight or more of them boxing as seniors in the club. That's a lot to have in one club, to be honest. I'm wondering, now, where they all came from."

It was a neat, powerfully delivered, left hook – so often the downfall of southpaws – that finally put paid to any hopes Bryan might still have harboured of retrieving the contest against Roche. It sent the Midlander reeling against the ropes.

"He was falling around and I rushed in to finish it and missed him. I couldn't believe it. But I unloaded three or four more shots after that and that was when the ref stepped in."

Still a little sore and aching a day or so after the fight and back in Leeds, Derek had said: "I was a bit rusty but I improved as the bout progressed. I'm relaxing for a few days now and I'm nursing a few stitches above the eye."

There was time to celebrate and Derek brought along his newly-won belt to Delaney's Bar for all to see. And needless to say there were many able to see it in double by the early hours of the next morning.

Where there is a winner, of course, there is also a loser and it was after that fight that Bryan decided it was time to call it a day.

Talking about the contest for this book, Derek recalls: "Sure, I was glad with the win and the belt but I was already wanting the next one. I'd also picked up that cut above the eye and had to have the eyebrow shaved to stitch up the wound, which was a bit annoying. I wasn't feeling as happy as I should."

It was now nearly 18 months since Derek's eliminator for the British title when he'd beaten Chris Saunders and he was eager to get on with matters.

"It's a bit weird boxing," says Derek, "you enjoy the win but then you want the next one to come along. I wanted to get things moving. I was in a hurry."

The victory over Bryan was another notable scalp in Derek's 19-fight undefeated pro career as well as being another title. Importantly too, the contest had been broadcast on the BBC – Derek's talents were at last being noticed after 11 stoppage wins in 89 rounds of paid fighting.

We got to talking one day about the media, in particular the BBC and other television stations, and the exposure that boxing receives. Derek is of the opinion that boxers rarely get the recognition that their achievements merit – at least compared to people in a lot of other sports.

We had rather wandered on to this subject. I had actually been wondering to myself how accurate a portrayal of Derek's character was coming over in what had already been written. Most people who meet Derek comment on what a likeable bloke he is. For sure, he is patient, quick-witted and has a lot of charm – qualities far removed from many people's idea of boxers.

But then again a lot of people's impressions of boxers in

recent years have been moulded by that most high profile of all fighters, Mike Tyson, or, perhaps more accurately, by his more outrageous antics.

Fabulous fighter though Tyson has undoubtedly been, he is hardly likely to land a job as boxing's chief standard bearer.

Derek grins. "Well I suppose you're right there, but to be honest Tyson was one of my inspirations to be a boxer – he's a real boxing hero of mine."

"Which other boxers have you particularly admired?" I ask.

"Well, Marvin Hagler's one and Roberto Duran's another. I liked them because they were brave, brave fighters, always coming forward. Exciting to watch."

Few could disagree with that.

Derek's own character comes back to my mind. The more you get to know him the more easily recognisable is the underlying steel within him. Call it hardness if you want. It is an important, possibly an essential, element in a boxer – a fighter needs more than just fitness and skill – to keep on going he needs heart. And you cannot teach that.

As a fight gets closer it is noticeable how Derek withdraws more into himself and that hardness of character becomes more evident. There are occasional glimpses of it at other times too.

An incident that serves as an illustration occurred in Delaney's bar one evening when Derek was on duty.

A loud-mouthed customer was sitting at a table, feet up on a chair, being a nuisance, and showing off to the two women with him. It needs to be said that the man was not your average, amiable, pub punter who had had one too many; he was a big man physically and clearly accustomed to having his own way.

Derek, in his capacity as a doorman, strolled over to have a polite word in his ear.

The man looked up, contempt oozing from his face.

"And who the fuck do you think YOU are?" he spat at Derek.

Derek said nothing for a moment but just stared with

unblinking eyes, leaning his head slightly back. Slowly he raised both hands to waist height and gently folded his fingers inwards. He spoke softly, but every word was delivered clearly and emphasised by his Wexford accent.

"Stand up and I'll SHOW you who the fuck I am," he said.

The troublemaker stared back. He was weighing up the situation. Suddenly his confidence visibly ebbed away. He forced a smile as if to ask what all the fuss was about, rubbed his nose and took his feet off the chair. Derek said nothing more but moved away slowly, allowing the man to keep what dignity he had left.

I mention this not to glorify Derek's approach and I daresay it was not an example of best practice in the Ladybird Guide to Door-Minding Etiquette, but it perhaps demonstrates a part of his make-up that is a vital ingredient of being a boxer.

Anyway, I relate none of this to Derek but just carry on talking about Duran, Hagler and other boxing heroes.

We chew over this topic for a while and being a bit – OK, quite a lot – older than Derek, I mention a boxer I always found exciting: Dave 'Boy' Green, known as the Fen Tiger.

Derek knows of him, though he cannot have been more than a few years old when Green won the British and European light-welterweight titles back in the mid-70s and the European welterweight title in 1979. Green, famed for his barnstorming style, also twice challenged for the WBC world welterweight title, losing to Carlos Palomino on his first attempt in 1977 and to American legend Sugar Ray Leonard in 1980.

By the time he called it a day Green had won 37 of his 41 fights with an incredible 29 stoppages to his credit.

I used to watch Green on TV.

And that is how we strayed on to the subject of the media.

Green was active at a time when boxing enjoyed huge exposure on television and in the press and many fighters were household names.

Looking back to the seventies it seems that just about anyone in Britain with even a passing interest in sport had heard of the likes of Joe Bugner, Ken Buchanan, John Conteh,

Henry Cooper, Jim Watt, Barry McGuigan and many, many more. The American greats like Ali, Foreman, Frazier and Norton were all world famous. Even today Ali is said to be still the most recognised man on the planet.

Nowadays, though, it seems that boxing's widespread appeal has dwindled – in the UK at least. That is not to say it does not still have a faithful following but very few boxers nowadays are what you might call household names.

Lennox Lewis and Prince Naseem are possibly the only boxers of late instantly recognised in Britain by the majority of people outside the sport. Audley Harrison is only a little way behind but Ricky Hatton, possibly Joe Calzaghe and one or two others have only recently begun to emerge into the general public's consciousness. Apart from Tyson, I would put money on the likes of other international stars such as Roy Jones, the Klitchkos, Bernard Hopkins, Oscar de la Hoya *et al* being names hardly heard of in the UK outside boxing circles.

The lack of exposure in the media has done little to help boxing, though it would seem that the tide has been turning in recent years. The BBC, for example, began showing a greater commitment to the sport after Audley Harrison won an Olympic gold medal in Sydney.

Harrison's contribution should not be underestimated and his achievement is doubtless more than a little responsible for the growth in the number of youngsters coming into the sport. His post-Olympic deal with the BBC after joining the paid ranks also helped deliver professional boxing to a wider audience. It seems a little odd then that Harrison attracted so much criticism about his fights, including criticism from within the fight game itself. To my mind, he embarked on a sensible enough path towards his target of a world title. No other boxer would expect to be thrown in at the deep end immediately after turning pro.

"My only criticism," says Derek, "would be that Audley should have been on the undercards rather than topping the bills at those early shows of his. Eventually, though, every boxer has to step it up and face good opposition if he's going to get anywhere. It's a learning process."

Undoubtedly, there was jealously among some people in the sport that Harrison should have enjoyed so much initial publicity as a pro compared to other boxers setting out. But then again how many others ever won an Olympic gold? Interestingly, though, Harrison's experience is in stark contrast to the reception offered Joe Frazier after he won an Olympic Gold in Tokyo for the United States. He beat German Hans Huber in the final and returned to America with a plaster cast on his hand having suffered a broken thumb. He then went back to work in a slaughterhouse, hosing away blood from the floor.

Because of the cast, though, he was unable to work properly and was eventually sacked from the job. Hardly any way to treat a hero, you would think. But that was a different era – different values.

Nowadays we live in the age of celebrity.

Audley Harrison is a big name and therefore inevitably he attracts a lot of interest and large television audiences. Harrison's success has helped resurrect boxing as a sport on the terrestrial television channels.

Undeniably, Sky does a fine job with its coverage of the sport but its audience is more limited than that of the BBC, the station being a satellite channel. The BBC has the potential to bring the sport to a much wider audience.

And when it does broadcast boxing, viewing figures reveal that the sport still has a great hold on the public imagination.

Sometimes, though, it must seem boxers appear overnight – one day they have hardly been heard of, the next day they are challenging for a major title. More recently the BBC has been showing more up-and-coming fighters.

Even so, it would be nice to see more newspapers and local television stations covering their local boxers and charting their progress. Giving boxers greater publicity would doubtless help them reap the rewards that all their work and dedication merit.

Derek himself has had a fair amount of publicity in the press but it has to be said not nearly as much as his achievements in the ring deserve. His experience is typical to that of many boxers throughout Britain. When you compare their exposure with that given to footballers, for example, it seems almost ludicrous.

But back in the pre-war days when newspaper sales were at their peak and TV, of course, hardly existed, boxing was afforded massive coverage in the press, including the numerous small-hall fights.

The world has changed, though, and the days of the small-hall boxing shows have faded.

To some extent, boxing does itself few favours. Whereas many sports nowadays are geared up to spoon-feed the press, boxing as an organisation seems to have failed to keep up with the pace.

Today's papers operate on much smaller editorial budgets than they once did, with fewer staff and as a consequence those sports prepared to invest in the likes of press officers and PR people end up with the lion's share of publicity.

If boxing is prepared to regard itself as a minority sport then that is the status it will eventually have to accept.

My own experience, by the way, is that people in boxing are the most approachable and friendly of all sports people and rarely less than co-operative.

But as an organised sport, chaos seems to reign despite the best efforts of a number of individuals.

In many ways, the anarchic aspect of boxing is to be admired – the very fact that fighters, trainers and promoters simply get on with the job regardless is a reflection of their dedication.

But the boxers themselves deserve a fair deal.

Generating publicity for the big events is easy enough if for no better reason than the media always loves a circus and feeds off celebrities.

For that reason, presumably, we have had at one end of the boxing spectrum some of the highest earning athletes in the world like Lewis and Naz, who make even Premiership soccer pin-ups look like paupers, while at the other end decent, but unsung, fighters are barely scraping by. It is the bread-and-butter end of the sport that needs special attention.

Some say the proliferation of confusing titles and an alphabet soup of awarding bodies has caused confusion among people who might otherwise be drawn to the sport. Of course, it is understandable that smaller promoters see some of the lesser titles as an opportunity to sell more tickets and obviously it is nice for fighters to win something, too. But in the long term the fear is that such awards might prove to be counter-productive. The argument is that the traditional titles are devalued simply because of the confusion created. Nowadays for example, as well as the European title we have the fairly recent European Union crown. The two have been confused by some sports journalists so it is hardly a surprise if the sporting public is bewildered too.

It is well worth remembering there are plenty of other, less perplexing, sports to follow.

On the other hand, at least the title fights offer competitive bouts; the number of contests whose outcome is all too predictable seems to be depressingly frequent, the consequence being that professional boxing could before long find itself in danger of being an imitation of the wrestling circus.

It does not mean that boxing will disappear; in the world of pay-for-view TV that offers 'top-name' showdowns there is always going to be an audience. But it means fight fans are more likely to be occasional supporters than die-hard aficionados and usually they will be less educated about the sport than their predecessors who frequented the small halls.

They will want to be entertained, though, and what that means is that boxers will be expected to bring more to the ring than just fighting skills and talent if they want to progress a long way. They will need to be showmen too.

Some might argue that it was ever so.

Perhaps it is of little surprise that there are some in the professional game who will secretly confide that their true heart still resides in the amateur game.

Chapter Sixteen

British crown and Irish party

APRIL 10 1999. The big day arrived. This was to be the culmination of years of toil and pain. The previous weeks had seen Derek work as hard as ever he had. The opportunity to wear the British belt was a chance he was determined should not slip away. Yet for 30-year-old opponent Charlie Kane the sentiment was the same.

The odds before the contest favoured the Scotsman – on paper at least. The Glasgwegian was tall and an accomplished, stylish southpaw, boasting an outstanding amateur pedigree. He had won a gold medal at the 1990 Commonwealth Games in New Zealand at light-welter. As a professional he had lost only once, that being to Ross Hale in 1995 when he challenged for the British and Commonwealth light-welter title. His chance of a Lonsdale belt, then, had already passed him by once.

He was determined that it would not happen again.

Naturally, Derek knew the task ahead was going to be no piece of cake. Originally he had expected to meet Geoff McCreesh for the crown but McCreesh had vacated the title which he had won from Kevin Leushing. It was generally thought that McCreesh would have been tailor-made for Derek and there were some, unfairly I would say, who reckoned McCreesh had vacated rather than face Rebel Roche.

The contest between Kane and Roche was a different proposition and promised to be a battle of contrasts – the southpaw boxer against the hard-hitting fighter.

Derek had studied the video tapes and his sparring had, not surprisingly, been against tallish southpaws. He knew Kane was sharp and he knew that he needed to get past Kane's jab and work on the inside, brawling at close quarters.

"A lot of things go through your mind when you're preparing for a fight," says Derek. "But I tend not to dwell too much on what the other bloke might do. I know what his options are so I concentrate on what I'm going to do. And I let him worry about that."

The preparations had been thorough but the only true test now was in the contest ring itself.

In Derek's corner were Kevin Spratt, John Celebanski and cutsman Benny King.

"John's always a good man to have around before a fight," says Derek. "He takes the pressure off with all his chat and comments. He makes it seem like just another day out and doesn't get wound up. If the people around you are getting nervous there's always the danger that they can pass that tension on. You need a bit of edginess, that's normal, but the best way is to stay calm, stay relaxed so you're not wooden when that bell rings."

There was good support for Derek as he climbed into the ring to the strains of the Irish pipes wearing his Irish green tartan kilt – his battle kit as he liked to call it.

Roche fans had travelled to Manchester's MEN Arena from Leeds and Ireland and up from Bournemouth.

Derek himself had sold £16,000 worth of tickets.

Kane, sporting blue shorts styled in the design of the Scottish saltire, was cheered to the ring by his own supporters down from Glasgow.

Both men had weighed in at 10 st 6lb.

Broadcast live on Sky Box Office, the main event of the evening, however, was not Kane v Roche but a showdown between two Yorkshiremen, Prince Naseem Hamed, of Sheffield defending his WBO featherweight title against Paul Ingle, of Scarborough.

Kane and Roche, though, were focused on their own personal Celtic battle.

Derek paced the ring like a caged tiger before being called to the centre by referee Roy Francis to touch gloves. Back to the corner. A nod and final comments from Spratt and then Derek was in there by himself.

Everything was now up to him.

Round One. Derek looks keen as he stalks his man. Kane as expected is wary, keeping his distance and weighing up his opponent. The highlight of the three-minutes is one well judged right uppercut from Derek that marks Kane under the left eye. Otherwise the round is too close to call – ten points apiece.

Round Two. Derek is trying to follow the game-plan and get close to Kane, prepared to "take one to land one" as he himself puts it. He makes a breakthrough with a right, followed by a left hook, with just under 50 seconds of the round to go and Kane goes down for a count of eight. Derek retreats to a neutral corner. He knows in himself though that Kane is by no means finished. Derek has trained for 12 rounds and if the contest has to go the full distance so be it.

Round Three. Kane seems untroubled after the knock-down, but is failing to dominate from range as he would have hoped. And then he produces a short left straight through the middle, sending Derek to the canvas and regaining parity on the scorecard. The knock-down is unsettling for the Roche camp as Kane is not a noted puncher. He has stopped just five of his 15 previous opponents.

Rounds Four, Five and Six. Throughout these rounds, Derek struggles in his attempts to work on the inside, with Kane understandably holding whenever Derek comes forward. Kane also begins to find his range from a distance and he bloodies Derek's nose. Derek is becoming frustrated and is wobbled by a good left from the Scotsman. The points are beginning to slip away from The Rebel with Kane's jab finding Derek's head with worrying regularity.

Round Seven. Derek knows this is a vital round. He can ill afford to let Kane get too far ahead with the fight now having passed the half-way stage. Derek responds with a good right and Kane slips down the ropes to the canvas. The Scotsman is up quickly, though, protesting that he has merely slipped. But referee Roy Francis rightly considers that it was Derek's punch that unbalanced him.

Derek's looking at a 10-8 round in his favour that will help claw back the points, assuming he can do enough for the remaining half of the seventh. But he goes further than that. A big right suddenly catches Kane on the button and this time there is no doubt as Glasgow's hero crashes to the canvas. Kane is sprawled out and for a moment looks like he will stay there. But suddenly something clicks in his mind, the boxer's grit and determination is still there, and he springs up on the count of nine to everyone's surprise and admiration. But referee Francis looks into his eyes. He has no hesitation. Kane's eyes have as much focus as glazed cherries. The fight is over.

A huge smile immediately breaks across Derek's face as he sees the referee's arms waving.

There is no protest from Kane. He knows his chance has gone and looks to the ground as Derek salutes the crowd with hands aloft.

Derek's dream of the British crown has just become reality.

Spratt, Celebanski and Tommy Gilmour are all in the ring to share Derek's joy as the result is announced.

At the age of 27, the Irishman from New Ross had added his name to a classic weight division title alongside such illustrious legends as John H. Stracey, Lloyd Honeyghan and many, many more.

As is the case in TV fights the pundits then get to have their say. There is understandable sympathy for Kane as well as congratulations for Derek.

One pundit suggests that Derek has triumphed with a "lucky" punch. Perhaps it is the TV man's intention to ease Kane's disappointment. But to use the word "lucky" strikes me as unjust. It is a cliché in sport. Sportsmen make their own luck. Derek had earned his right to be in that ring, the punch was thrown with intent and landed. Kane would have known that Derek's heavy right hand was the most potent weapon in his armoury yet he was tagged by it. Ahead on points Kane might well have been, as a stylist that was always going to be on the cards. But in boxing it only takes one punch and Derek had found it when it was needed.

Derek said after the fight: "He was so awkward and he held

me inside so I didn't get a chance to work inside, which is where I'm strongest. But every time I was hitting and hurting him a bit. He was trying to cover it up but I could see through him."

It was party time once more at Delaney's Bar.

Looking back at his victory a few years later, Derek says the win failed to sink in immediately.

"It was a great feeling but I think I actually feel prouder about it now than I did at the time. Well, not exactly prouder, it's just that perhaps I appreciate the achievement more after all this time. I remember a few days after the fight I went back to Ireland with the belt and that was nice. We just went to relax a bit. I went with Kevin and we flew into Dublin. Dad and Uncle Pat picked us up at the airport to take us back to New Ross. We stopped at a pub in a village about 20 miles away and just had a couple of pints. It felt good to be going home. Then we pulled into the Bosheen and I suddenly saw everyone had turned out to welcome me back."

The whole area was strewn with bunting in the Irish colours. All the streets had turned out and the local shops were giving out free sweets to the youngsters and the pubs had free beer.

In the centre of the Bosheen is a green where there was an open-backed lorry from where dignitaries, including the local priest welcomed Derek home.

"It was one big party," says Derek. "I can't find the words to describe how I felt. There was a lump in my throat and I thought I was going to burst into tears. Then I turned round and Kevin was actually crying."

Everyone wanted to talk to Derek and tell him how they had watched the fight and seen him win on television.

He was told all four local pubs with the means to show the fight had been full to bursting on the night. When the TV in one of the pubs had lost reception during the contest the pub had emptied in an instant as every one of the drinkers rushed across the road to force their way into the nearest bar still broadcasting the battle.

"Everyone was shaking my hand and treating me like some hero that day I came back."

A photograph of that memorable day featuring a beaming Derek holding aloft his Lonsdale belt and flanked by his mum and dad graces the opening page of Barnie Eastwood's *Irish Boxing Yearbook 2000.* It is a clear tribute to the esteem that was felt for Derek in his native Ireland.

His achievement seems to have touched the hearts of everyone. He still has a letter from the Very Reverend Jack McCabe. It reads: *Dear Derek, I would like to take this opportunity to offer on behalf of the priests and people of the Parish our congratulations on your recent success.*

As I said in the Bosheen on Tuesday, the dedication and discipline needed on such an achievement cannot be understood unless experienced.

I wish you continued success and hope we will have many more proud days in the Bosheen.

Yours sincerely, The Very Rev Jack McCabe.

After the celebrations of the Bosheen, Derek was taken to the neighbouring Mount Carmel estate where all the youngsters were kitted out in traditional Irish costumes and waving the tricolour.

"They'd all turned out just to see me," says Derek, almost in disbelief.

Later in the week there was a civic reception in the town's main civic building the Tholsel for Derek and the local Gaelic football team that had won an All-Ireland trophy.

"It was all nice, really nice," recalls Derek. "It means a lot when your own people go to such an effort for you. I will always remember it all because I wasn't expecting anything. I thought we'd be just going down the pub."

Chapter Seventeen

Fighting crime in different ways

DEREK walking his dog is a sight that might make many people cross the road to get out of the way. Derek's a boxer by trade, Buster a boxer by breed. They are both laid back by nature but you would probably not think so to look at them.

So the Leeds mugger who clocked on for business the morning Derek and Buster were taking a little stroll had presumably failed to see them or had taken one-too-many dumb-down tablets.

It was broad daylight and the 82-year-old lady should have felt safe as she shuffled towards the shops. But it was still early and quiet and she must have looked an easy target.

"I couldn't believe it," said Derek. "This bloke just ran up to the old lady and grabs her purse. She tries to hang on to it but he drags her to the ground. I just let go of Buster's leash and chased after him."

It did not take Derek long to catch up.

"I rugby tackled him from behind and he went flying over this wall. I know that you read about people doing things by instinct but that's just what it was for me. I didn't have time to think. It was instinct. I just saw this poor old lady getting robbed and I thought, 'right, you bastard' and went after him.

"After I tackled him and he went over the wall I went and grabbed him. I didn't punch him or nothing, just got him in a headlock and held on tight. He was shouting at me something like 'let me go, mate it wasn't me, I done nothing.'

"But I'd seen him and I saw him throw the woman's purse behind him when I caught him. I mean how could he hurt an old lady like that? I don't know. He started struggling, so I just squeezes him round the neck a little tighter, that settled him down. Someone else went to see the old lady and I kept hold of the fella till the police comes along.

"This other bloke then suddenly comes down a ladder off the roof and asks me matter-of-fact like: 'Are you all right there son?'

"That was kind of comical.

"I don't know what he thought I was doing. Anyhow when the cops come this policewoman asks me a few questions and that, and then she comes to my house a bit later on and writes a few things down. She's making sure I don't say I've beaten him up or anything, which I hadn't anyhow."

He pauses. "That's true, that is. I think she said she'd have had to arrest me or something if I had punched him or whatever, which I thought was a bit funny. But there you go."

Much to Derek's surprise, the incident was to earn him more newspaper coverage than most of his fights in the ring. There were headlines in many of the nationals both in Britain, Ireland and even America – with Derek feted as a hero. The idea of a callous villain being handed out a bit of his own medicine, clearly struck a universal chord.

Happily, the elderly victim recovered from her physical injuries but who can measure the psychological scarring?

Derek's actions were officially recognised when he was presented with the Divisional Commander's Commendation by West Yorkshire Police. Making the presentation was Chief Superintendent Keith Lawrence.

"It was a bit ironical," Derek recalls. "I was invited down to Killingbeck Police Station for the ceremony. The last time I'd been there, they'd put me in a cell then driven me up to Scotland."

He laughs.

After the presentation Derek had said: "I suppose it's nice to be recognised and praised for doing the right thing. I feel very honoured and pleased."

There is often a thin dividing line between being on the right side or the wrong side of the law. By apprehending a mugger Derek was commended; had he used a bit too much force in tackling him he could have been condemned. It is a grey area – open to interpretation, if you like.

So when Derek talks of another incident, he makes sure he speaks carefully. It was after he had met Tracei and they were living in the Gipton area of Leeds. Derek came home after training to find a break-in at their house. The front door had been forced and nearly all the stuff they had saved for and bought was gone.

"I felt mad. Real mad," said Derek. "When I saw Tracei crying it just made me boil inside. I got into the car and went around to see a few of the 'Big Men' in the area. Find out who knew what. One of them gave me a clue so I raced round to this house. He was a smackhead. But it was an ol' fella who comes to the door. I tell him to tell his son he's got half-an-hour to bring all my stuff back."

Derek rubs his chin.

"So's after 25 minutes a van with all my stuff screeches up outside my house. This smackhead gets out and starts grinning, trying to tells me there's been a bit of a misunderstanding. Anyhow, I explain to him in terms that the bastard can understand that I'm not best pleased. I also persuade him in a way that he understood that I wanted the cash to repair the damage he'd done to my door."

Chapter Eighteen

A Lonsdale belt to keep

DEREK'S first defence of the British title – on July 31, 1999 – was in Carlisle, three months after his victory over Kane. His opponent this time was Basildon's Georgie Smith who had lost just two of his 19 fights – one to Charlie Kane and the other to Russian super-featherweight champion Rimvidus Bilius, though he had later avenged this defeat.

Carlisle is rarely noted for thermometer-bursting heatwaves but this mid-summer evening it was sweltering as Derek climbed into the ring.

"It was really, really hot," says Derek – hardly ideal conditions for a 12 rounder. In the end the fight did indeed go the distance. It marked the first full 12 competitive rounds Derek had completed.

It is not an achievement that should be underestimated. Boxers can spar 12 rounds or more in the gym but going the distance in the competitive ring is the only way to prove a fighter has enough in the tank to last the full 36 minutes.

"Well, I proved to myself I could do it," says Derek, "but in that heat it wasn't easy. I don't know what the temperature must have been but what with the lights and the weather we were both just pouring sweat.

"I felt completely dehydrated by the end. Twelve rounds take a lot out of you – it takes a lot longer to recover than fighting say four six-rounders over a short space of time. But it was a pleasing win.

"To be honest going into the fight I thought I'd knock out Georgie. He was one of Barry Hearns' blue-eyed boys and he was very tough that night. It wasn't his punching power, though, that impressed me. He had a bit of a reputation as a hard hitter but I didn't find he was punching that hard on the night. There again, I hit him with some real shots and was a bit shocked to see he was still there. So he was a tough un."

Smith had gone a full 12 rounds before, notably in that return against Rimvidus Bilius the previous year when he had clinched the vacant IBO Inter-Continental welterweight title.

"Sometimes it's easy to lose track over 12 rounds," said Derek. "I had to look at the ring girls and was surprised to see it was the ninth round because I'd thought it was the 11th. But when you're in there you're so focused on the fight that it's very easy to lose track because you cut out everything else from your mind but the fella in front of you. It's like with the crowd – once you're fighting you're not really aware of them, occasionally someone shouting something out to you penetrates but it's a kind of background noise at the time, even if you remember it afterwards. Hard to explain, really but there's a lot of concentration when you're fighting. I've said it before, and it's true you know, the concentration can be more exhausting than the actual physical exertion."

Derek, though, came through the 12-round test with flying colours for a points win – a victory that was a belated if hard-earned gift less than two weeks after his 27th birthday.

For Smith the outcome was different – he decided to call it a day after meeting Roche, doubtless believing there was only one direction to go if he stayed in boxing after that defeat and it was not going to be upwards.

Team Roche, though, had plenty to celebrate and Kevin Spratt is not one to let the chance of a party pass by.

After the celebrations, following the win over Smith, it was quickly back to business with Derek preparing for his next defence, this time an encounter with talented Scotsman Scott Dixon. That battle came less than three months after the Smith fight.

Derek was all too aware that Dixon was a dangerous opponent.

"I've always gone into any fight confident of winning and Dixon was no exception but I knew he was tough and durable and that he deserved respect. He was stronger than Kane had been but then again not as classy either."

Dixon had lost only once, that being a defeat over 12 rounds in Dublin against Michael Carruth for the vacant WAA welter crown. Earlier that year he had won the WBB title, stopping Edwin Murillo in the sixth round at the York Hall in Bethnal Green, London.

After fighting Derek he was to go on to clinch the Commonwealth and Scottish welterweight titles.

But few could have predicted before the clash that by the end of 12 punishing rounds the Roche v Dixon contest would be judged as having been one of the best matches of the decade.

On paper it had looked like being a clash of styles: the dancer versus the brawler.

Dixon at six foot tall was expected to use his height and reach advantage to jab from a distance and box off the back foot, out of Roche's range.

These were all the ingredients for a dull stalemate rather than a thrilling spectacle.

There was no doubting, though, that both fighters were hungry to win; Dixon, just as Kane had been, was desperate to take the title back to Scotland while for Roche the chance to secure that Lonsdale belt outright was now within his grasp.

The two warriors climbed into the ring at Coventry, Dixon in blue shorts and Derek once more in his battle kit – the Wexford kilt.

Dixon's eight weeks of preparation had been thorough, including 6,000 sit-ups and thousands more chin-ups, as well as mile upon mile of gruelling roadwork.

The television commentators made much of Dixon's training programme, something that still puzzles Derek as he says that his own preparations had more than equalled those of Dixon.

Shaved into Dixon's haircut were the words Super Scot, or possibly Super Scott – the back of a man's head is not always the ideal medium for calligraphy.

The two fighters squared up and Dixon looked both confident and agile as he circled Derek, testing his range. Then, with less than two minutes of the first round gone, Derek was sent crashing to the canvas by a flashing left hook to the chin.

It was a shock but the Irishman sprang back to his feet with no obvious signs of being hurt.

The TV commentator, Ian Darke, noted that Roche "normally gets up to stop his opponent."

Dixon had been sparring with West Ham cruiserweight Garry Delaney in a bid to cope with Derek's strength. He put the preparation to good effect in the second to take that round too. Though throwing more punches, far fewer of Derek's shots had landed, and it was a similar story in the third with Dixon blocking most of Derek's punches. Rather than moving out of range, though, Dixon seemed confident enough to stand his ground.

It was a scrappier round but Derek was now four points adrift and was failing to grind his opponent down, or as former WBC lightweight champion and Sky Sports pundit Jim Watt put it: "do anything clever."

The fourth was a close affair but Dixon still managed to land his left and Derek seemed unable to open up his man. It was becoming hard to see how Derek might spoil Dixon's record of never having been put down before and in the fifth the Scotsman took most of what Derek had to offer on the arms or shoulders. Then, with little more than 20 seconds to go before the end of the three minutes, Roche caught Dixon with a firm right and followed up with a left hook to the temple. Dixon stepped, or more accurately stumbled out of range, teetered for a moment and then, as if someone had just unplugged the mains, his legs collapsed beneath him.

"We said don't write off Roche," bellowed Darke.

Bravely, though, Dixon hauled himself up on the count of eight and the bell rang before Derek was able to unload any fight-finishing blows.

Dixon needed that full minute in his corner to regain his senses and was doubtless happy in the sixth to be given a further respite when a lace came loose on Roche's glove, requiring tape from Kevin Spratt in the corner.

Derek was now firing powerful shots but Dixon responded with shots of his own, before a hard left to the body from Roche sneaked in under the elbow thumping into the short rib and deflating Dixon who sank to the canvas like a folding parachute.

But there were just 13 seconds of the round to go and, though Dixon somehow found the strength to stand up and beat the count, it was the bell that once more came to his rescue. Again he was given a full 60 seconds to try to regain his senses.

In round seven, though, Roche's glove again came loose, requiring hasty remedial work in the corner before both men took to the centre of the ring and traded frenzied punches.

Roche smiled as he took a blow – not always a good sign. Again Dixon flashed out a left hook and wobbled Derek who suddenly found himself having to fight on instinct as he tried to clear his scrambled senses.

The fighting swung to and fro before Roche landed a heavy combination. Now Dixon seemed rattled and ready to topple. Instead he turned Roche and lashed out.

"That," enthused Jim Watt, "was one of the best rounds of boxing I've seen in recent times."

Round eight and there was still everything to fight for.

"It might come down to who wants the title more," said the commentator.

Roche was now looking for the body. Dixon replied with an uppercut. Roche beckoned him in and both men answered fire with fire but it looked as if Roche had just edged that round.

Into round nine and it was evident that Derek's right eye was beginning to close but his sight seemed as yet unaffected. Then halfway through the round he found Dixon's ribs again with a crippling right and Dixon sank to the canvas once more.

This time, it seemed, there was no way back for the Scotsman, yet, almost unbelievably, he again struggled to his feet and referee Dave Parris brought the pair together to box on. Even more remarkably, Dixon began to unload on Derek.

He turned him on to the ropes and lashed out with a fierce left hook. Boom. Derek takes it on the right glove. Boom. A second left hook. Derek is rooted to the spot. Boom. A third left. Boom. A fourth. This time the shot bypasses Derek's glove and lands on his chin. Down goes The Rebel.

It is the second knock down of the round and the fifth of the contest.

Dazed, but not out, Roche made it back to his feet and nodded to the ref, indicating he was OK to carry on. Blood was now running from his nose.

Into the tenth and Dixon looked the stronger of the two.

This should have been Derek's territory but he was having to hold and cling on, desperate to survive.

Then suddenly back he came, pulling out a right that wobbled Dixon. But again the Scotsman replied and the streaming blood from Derek's eye caused the ref to lead the Irishman to his corner for a check.

It was feared it might be over but Parris then signalled for the fight to continue. It would have been a cruel way to stop such a contest.

The chance was there, possibly, for Dixon to force a stoppage, but for reasons known only to himself he seemed to ease off, take his foot off the pedal and Derek made it to the end of the round allowing cutsman Benny King a precious minute to ply his magic.

The fight at this stage seemed evenly balanced. Some of the rounds had been hard to call so it all depended on how the ref had seen it.

Roche, though, then worked harder in round 11, and there was no doubting he won that one. Still the result was in doubt, but in the 12th, it was the Rebel Roche who dug the deepest, drawing on his reserves of courage to take that round too.

At the bell though, there was enough uncertainty to bring the iciest of gamblers out in a sweat. Parris, though, allowed no time for speculation, immediately raising Derek's arm in victory.

Dixon looked devastated. A wave of disappointment

seemed to visibly sweep through his body. Clearly he thought he had done enough to have got the nod.

The score, though, gave Derek a three-round advantage: 114 points to 117.

It might seem that that was a little generous but my own verdict, for what it is worth, was that Derek had done enough in those final two rounds to clinch it.

After the fight the TV boys quizzed the two warriors and Derek said he thought he might have lost it. It is rare that you hear a boxer say something like that. He said he thought he was behind going into the last three minutes. He also paid tribute to Scott for beating the count after the body shots.

"I thought no way will he get up," said Derek.

Of the second punch that had put Dixon down, he added: "You could feel the shot going into the body and I didn't think he'd get up."

Dixon, clearly still disappointed at the result, managed to congratulate Derek and it was hard not to feel sorry for the man after his Titanic efforts.

But I have studied the tape time and again since and my conclusion remains the same – Derek did indeed win the fight.

I have the score even going into the 11th and as Derek most definitely won both those last couple of rounds that means he won the contest by two at the final bell on my reckoning.

His corner, though, had told him he was behind going into the last – but that, of course, would have been to gee Derek up for a final effort.

Dixon's corner had told their man he was ahead – presumably they believed that and they wanted Scott to keep out of danger, to avoid a KO blow from the Irishman.

At the end of the day, of course, it is the judges' or referee's decision that counts. Even if scoring rounds can be tough, it has to be said that Derek deserved the fight if only on the basis of having scored more knock-downs and finishing the fight the strongest.

Victory for Derek meant that in less than 12 months he had

earned himself an Inter-Continental title, the British crown and he was now an outright holder of a coveted Lonsdale belt. He was the first Irishman to win the Lonsdale belt outright – an achievement that still means a great deal to him.

"That's something no-one can take away," he says. "And yes I am proud to have won it. It means a lot."

It was time to celebrate.

The whole globe, of course, was celebrating soon after as mankind welcomed the dawn of a new millennium.

Chapter Nineteen

Marking the millennium

THE new millennium was marked around the world. In Australia, the waters of Sydney harbour reflected a sky lit by countless fireworks, bursting with almost divine glory as crowds gasped in awe at the scintillating spectacle. In Paris, the Eiffel Tower seemed to come to life, its gold-gilded girders glowing as if touched by the beating wings of an angel. People around the planet embraced and wept, moved to tears by the majesty of the moment.

In Leeds, Derek spat out a gobful of blood.

"I'd taken Tracei down into town to see in the New Year and we were in a bar near the railway station. I wasn't looking for any trouble, and that's for sure. I like Tracei to enjoy herself and that doesn't involve seeing me in a scrap when we go out, does it?"

The city centre was throbbing, though. With an explosive cocktail of contrived jollity and industrial quantities of beer, trouble was always threatening to erupt.

Derek and Tracei were sitting down at a table in the bar when he suddenly felt an empty bottle hit him on the back of the leg, having been kicked off the floor by some young yob across the room.

Derek turned his head, no more than mildly irritated, and saw the culprit, aged 19 or so, smirking. Derek sat down, shook his head, and having picked up the empty bottle, placed it on his table for collection by the bar staff.

He then had a sip on his own drink and wham... but it was not the alcoholic kick in the beer that sent him reeling.

"The lad I'd seen boot the beer bottle had come up behind me and whacked me on the side of the jaw. I didn't know him and I'll tell you to this day I've no idea why he came up and hit me. To be honest it wasn't a good punch to say that it was a free shot. It rattled my teeth a bit and cut the inside of me cheek, though."

Derek rubs his jaw while talking as if recalling the pain of the incident.

"Anyway, when I look around again the lad's legged it and I'm thinking 'well isn't this just a great way to be seeing in the new millennium?' Tracei says that we'd be best moving on so we decide to go.

"When we gets outside it turns out the bouncers have collared the lad who hit me and given him to the police. And there he is trying to wrestle himself free from a couple of coppers. One of them says to me something like: 'Is this the fella as hit you?' I tell him it is, because it was."

The officer then asked Derek if he wanted to make a complaint and have his attacker prosecuted.

"I'm thinking, what's he talking about? I says to your policeman: Listen, if you want to prosecute him, you prosecute him. I'll sort it out my own way. Then the copper turns on me and tells me either I make a complaint or that's it. And he growls at me that I'd better not start anything or I'll be in bother myself.

"I nods to him and then says, 'I'll be going now.' Then I turn round and says again that I'll sort it out myself. Anyhow Trace and myself are walking down near O'Reilly's Bar on Boar Lane. And guess who I see? It's only the lad who'd hit me – the coppers had already let him go. So I'm thinking, well guess what it is I'm thinking? Tracei's yelling: 'Come back Derek.'

"That's kind of romantic really, don't you think?

"Anyhow, your man goes to hit me – bad mistake – and I put him down with just the one shot. His pal then grabs me from the back. Well, now I'm really getting a bit sick of all this and I just throw back my head, crack, straight into his nose, splat, and he's down on the ground too. I'm ready now if they still want it, but they've had enough. They're both just lying there, groaning. Next thing, I'm groaning, too, 'cos who's plodding across the road in my direction but the same coppers who'd been talking to me before.

"And they were not best pleased, I'm afraid. The older one's glaring at me. I just say to him: 'I told yous I'd sort it out.'

"I bet he kept me down at the station for an extra hour or so because of me saying that. Anyhow it was 2.30 in the morning before they let me out. I missed all the millennium celebrations and that. I also had to promise that I wouldn't get into any more trouble. It was one of them, what do you call them? They bound me over to be of good behaviour, or something. And to be honest I have been of good behaviour. Because I don't go out looking for trouble, you know that."

Derek sits back, fold his arms and then remembers a further chat he once had with members of Her Majesty's constabulary.

"There was another time when I upset them, now I think about it. But that wasn't my fault, not at all. I was with Tracei again, would you believe it? It was getting late and we were at the taxi rank and there's a long line of people waiting."

The incident happened in a street outside the Majestyks nightclub in City Square, made famous by a few former Leeds United players.

"There was a police paddy van opposite, as it happens. Anyhow, a cab comes in and I wave my hand out. Suddenly, there's this big fella next to me saying that it's not my turn and that he's in front of me. I says that's OK, I'm not trying to push in or nothing, just, you know, sticking my hand out for the cabs to see us. Well, he shuts up for a minute and then off he starts moaning again, drinking from his bottle and I'm thinking to myself, 'here we go.' But Tracei grabs me and we move away from the queue, just waiting for it to thin out. Then the bloke, he comes up again. He starts shouting and we move away again. He follows us. It's the bully thing, you know, we're backing down, trying to be nice so he thinks he's got the better of us and won't give up. You see it all the time. Bully mentality, it is. And then he goes for it, lifts up the bottle and tries to slug me with it. Well, there's only so much I'm going to take."

Derek stops for a second.

"Wham and down he goes," continues Derek. "To be honest, I think everyone in the taxi-rank was happy. But then guess what happens. Up the police comes running, one big fella, big as an Irish gard he is, and another one. Anyhow, I can't believe it but they tell me they want to charge me with assault or something.

"'Aw come on boys,' I says, 'he was trying to knock me head off with that bottle. I just punched him the once.' But they wouldn't listen, of course, at least the big copper wouldn't and they marched me across to the paddy wagon and they threw me into the back. And I mean threw me.

"Anyhow I can hear them talking. The big copper's really got it in for me. I'm thinking he doesn't like my accent or something – well, I wasn't too happy with his face as it happens, the big, ugly bugger. He had big cauliflower ears he had, like he must have played rugby. The other one's telling him that everyone in the taxi queue has said it was me who was attacked so all I'd been doing was acting in self defence.

"The big copper's still not happy about it though and he keeps saying he wants to do me but the other one is saying he can't. It seemed to go on for ages like that.

"Finally they open the door and the big man says: 'right you, out.' He doesn't look happy, mind and he says: 'Now fuck off home before I change my mind.' "

Chapter Twenty

Losing the title and changing trainers

AFTER winning the Lonsdale belt outright, Derek had reached a stage in his career which might well have been a turning point. A shot at the European title might have been a sound option but such matters are rarely in the hands of boxers themselves. Managers have to consider the future of all their fighters, weigh up who gets a tilt at what and what deals can be struck.

After Dixon, Derek himself felt in no mood to relinquish his British crown, though it was to be nearly six months before he fought again. His challenger this time was to be Gravesend-born Harry Dhami, bidding to become the first boxer of Asian extraction to win a British title.

Derek said: "The six-months after Scott Dixon gave me a chance to have a rest, a chance to recharge the batteries. Looking back though, I guess I was becoming a bit over-confident. I was beginning to think I couldn't lose. I know that I underestimated Dhami."

Dhami had a mixed record. Coming into the fight he had lost four times in 18 outings, though all those defeats had come on the back of each other early in his career. Turning pro in 1992 at the age of 20, his second fight was more than a year-and-a-half after his debut. His string of losses suggested the career of a journeyman was all he could hope for. His attitude to the sport, however, seems to have changed dramatically when he won the Southern Area welterweight title, stopping Ojay Abrahams in five rounds in London. He successfully defended that belt four times before meeting Derek and had won his previous ten fights, building up a very worthy reputation along the way.

"It's not that I didn't take the fight seriously, but I didn't expect Dhami to trouble me at all," says Derek.

"Maybe I could have done with Kevin pushing me a bit harder in training at that time but I don't think he ever thought I'd have any difficulties. I guess we were all getting a bit too confident.

"I remember having a bust up at the gym with Kevin before the bout. He'd invited a few people down to see me sparring and they were stood around the ring drinking beer, laughing and smoking cigars. I didn't say anything at the time because I didn't want to embarrass Kev in front of his friends but I had a go at him in the changing room straight after. He knew I wasn't pleased but I think he thought he was doing a bit of the PR work or whatever you want to call it.

"We'd had it good so far me and Spratty and we thought things were going to get even better. The thing is you've got to win for that to happen. You've got to keep your eye on the target."

That training room row was a sign of more differences to come between Derek and Kevin. Had Derek beaten Dhami, it might just have all been forgotten but the Dhami showdown was to be the first time Derek tasted defeat in what was his 23rd start as a professional.

The contest was just down the road in Barnsley on March 27 2000. Although he lost his title that night, his performance in many ways provided an insight into what it means to be a fighter as Derek completed another 12 rounder – his third on the trot.

Nine of those rounds were fought with Derek in intense pain and unable to breathe properly after a heavy shot pulverised the bone and cartilage inside his nose.

The damage was done in round three. Derek had put Dhami on the canvas with a right hand before being caught himself with a bone-crushing shot.

"I knew I was in trouble because the pain was tremendous. I just couldn't breathe through my nose anymore. Every time I got hit I could hear it, at least it seemed to me I could actually hear my nose squelching. The agony was unbelievable. I didn't tell Spratty, though, because I thought he'd pull me out if he knew how bad it was. There were nine rounds to go and I was under pressure all of the time. Remember my style of fighting is being willing to take one to get one through but I was in so much pain I wasn't able to do that."

Derek was knocked to the canvas five times, but each time managed to convince the referee he was still fit to carry on.

It was an extreme example of a boxer hitting 'the wall' but against all the odds refusing to give in; battling on despite the odds. Critics might call such courage foolhardy but most I suspect would find it hard not to harbour at least a spark of admiration for such bravery.

"It's what you have to do," shrugs Derek.

"But the reason I kept being put down was I kept getting hit on the back of the head so often. To be fair, though, that was partly my fault because of the pain I was having I was keeping my nose out of the way and coming in low with my head down. I couldn't fight my normal fight. After six or seven rounds everyone was wondering why I kept looking for a knock-out punch.

"It's just I wanted to get it finished and over with. I'll admit that at one point I didn't think I could last a full 12 rounds but I kept trying. After a while I nearly accepted defeat but then I just thought to myself at least he won't stop me or knock me out.

"In the end I lost on points and that first loss was the hardest one for me. It was a real sickener – a blow to my pride."

The final verdict was 116-109 and the defeat meant that Derek saw his chances of a challenge for the European title evaporate.

Hardip Dhami paid tribute after the contest saying of Derek: "He was a true champion, he did not let it go easily. But it is my time now."

Derek's first thoughts were of a re-match.

"I wanted to fight him again," he recalled. "Straight away if possible. He'd said he'd love a re-match. I knew it would be a different story if we fought again."

Soon after the encounter Derek had said: "If he was as good as everyone is making out he should've been able to finish me off, but he couldn't. I was upset at the result but pleased I went the distance."

Derek was never to get that second chance against Dhami. Boxing rarely works out like that.

The pain of his injuries was outweighed only by the psychological pain of defeat. It was the physical injury, though, that put Derek in hospital.

He was in Leeds General Infirmary for five days after the contest. "I had this huge blood clot up my nose. The doctors lanced it and then shoved all this wadding up my nose. After a few days they pulled it all out and I'm not kidding, it was the worst sensation I've ever had. It hurt a bit but it wasn't that that bothered me so much, it was the sensation. It felt like everything in my head was draining out through my nose. It was a horrible feeling."

The five days in hospital gave Derek ample time to reflect on matters.

There is an old lament among boxers: 'First your head goes, then your legs go and in the end your friends go.'

Well, Derek, despite the defeat, had lost neither his head nor his legs but during his stay in hospital he received few visitors. "I guess I was feeling a bit sorry for myself," he says.

I tell Derek that I suspect people might have been reluctant to visit him in hospital not because they did not sympathise with his injuries but because they felt they had no place intruding on his grief after losing the title. Without wanting to sound flippant, I suggest it is perhaps not all that dissimilar to people finding it hard to talk to those who have suffered bereavement for fear of saying the wrong thing.

Derek, raises an eyebrow and looks a lot less than convinced by my amateur psychology.

He says that it hurt that Kevin never came to see him in hospital. "We'd enjoyed the good times together so I thought he could have come and shared a bad one too."

It was while in hospital that Derek decided that his professional partnership with Kevin had reached the end of the road.

"I don't think I ever considered quitting boxing but I decided I was going to move on with a new trainer.

"I think Spratty took the split badly at first but I'd made up my mind. I still think of him as a pal, don't get me wrong, and we'd had a lot of good times together. He's a good bloke. I think he was bitter about my decision to split but it's not one I took lightly – I'd been thinking about it for a little while because I felt we'd gone as far together as we could in the professional game. It was a professional decision, though I guess the disappointment in the hospital was the thing that tilted the balance."

Observing the situation from the outside it would be unfair to make any judgement except perhaps to say that in all professional sports such decisions are not unusual and not infrequent.

Happily, Kevin is now enjoying plenty of success in the promoting game.

Chapter Twenty-One

The real hands of Stone

FOLLOWING his split with trainer Kevin Spratt, Derek was assigned to Mark McCreath.

Bradford-born McCreath had a creditable record as a fighter (17 wins/seven defeats) and had boxed the majority of his bouts in mainland Europe. He twice contested the European light-welter title – once in 1991 when he lost to Brian Hughes-trained Pat Barrett and then, in 1993, when he lost to African-born Frenchman Valery Kayumba. Mark, though had won the Benelux welterweight title in Belgium in 1991, stopping Belgian Freddy Demeulenaere in the fifth round.

Roche and McCreath got their partnership off the blocks with a six-round points victory over Brian Coleman in Barnsley – a fight mentioned earlier in this book.

It might have been expected that a few more warm-up fights would follow before the new double-act contemplated a title shot. Boxing, though, has a habit of delivering the unexpected and a mere six weeks after beating journeyman Coleman, Derek found himself climbing into the ring for a world title tilt. He was to face Adrian Stone for the IBO light-middleweight crown.

I arranged a meeting with Derek in Delaney's Bar shortly before the looming encounter. With him, a little to my surprise, was the posse of Team Roche.

Derek himself seemed in sombre mood.

In contrast, Mark McCreath's jaw was firing on all cylinders. I remember Mark rattling off his sentences and sorely testing my shorthand speed to such an extent I welcomed the break when my pen ran out of ink. But Mark's a nice bloke to talk to, or more accurately to listen to. His enthusiasm is second to none.

Anyway, he poured praise on Derek that night.

"His co-ordination, his movement, his defence – every aspect of his boxing has improved," said Mark. "Even his punching power – and it's never been in doubt that Roche boasts a big dig – is stronger. He's kicking like a mule."

Joe Delaney chipped in as Mark paused for breath.

"Derek's got a punch like a sledgehammer," he said reminding me of what Charlie Kane had said that he had never been hit as hard before his fight with Derek.

Joe then came up with a first paragraph for the preview of the Adrian Stone showdown but suggested it be attributed to Derek.

"I'm going to show that you can get blood from a Stone."

I quite liked it and asked Derek if it was OK to use it as a quote. Derek seemed hardly to be listening but nodded.

Mark was soon eulogising once more.

"I believe this man has the heart of the great. I truly, truly believe that."

As if not to be outdone, Joe came back again: "Life hasn't always thrown too many favours in the direction of the Irish, particularly those abroad, but it has been with hard work and endeavour that we've shown the world what the Irish are capable of."

Mark nodded enthusiastically.

Joe carried on: "In Derek's profession, his efforts have now taken him to the brink of a world crown. I've been with Derek at every fight and I will be there with him when he wins his world title."

His eyes twinkled and then he winked and reminded me that the following sentence was a vital one: "We'll be showing off that world title in Delaney's Bar very soon."

Well, you could not help but admire his style.

Derek, I noticed had said little and looked weary. He did not seem quite right but I put that down to pre-fight edginess. Or maybe he just could not get a word in edgeways

It was only later that I was to discover that Derek had been unhappy with his training programme.

"It hadn't been going well," said Derek later. "I'm not

knocking Mark because he's a nice bloke and I still consider him a friend. But in the gym it didn't work for me.

"That's not to say Mark's not a good trainer with the right type of boxer. I wasn't the man for him and vice-versa, simple as that. Mark had been a good boxer himself. It's probably that he thought I should box to the same style that he did. I don't know. I'm a different type of fighter than he was.

"He'd have me looking in the mirror slightly adjusting the angle of my head to throw punches. It was getting me down. Another problem was that we didn't have a proper gym. We were travelling around using different gyms. I don't blame Mark for that but for a while we were using a cellar. I had a world title fight coming up and I was in a bloody cellar.

"You've got to be settled for a fight. Get your head together not worrying about where you're going to be the next day.

"I'm not knocking Mark because he doesn't deserve it and I know he was upset when we split up after that Stone fight. But there you go, that's what happened."

There was another problem for Derek that he, not surprisingly, neglected to mention to me before the fight and that was that he was nursing five stitches in his mouth – down the bottom lip to his lower gum – sustained in a head bang during sparring.

"That wasn't too great for me. The other thing on my mind was that Tracei had just had the baby. I wanted to be at home with them. All in all it was getting to me. I had the biggest fight of my life and for the first time in my career I wasn't looking forward to it."

The contest, at Belfast's Waterfront Hall, was for Stone's IBO light middleweight title and both fighters had agreed to come in at under 10st 10lb.

The date was November 11 2000 and was the main bout on the Sky television bill.

Stone, who, coincidentally, shares the same birthday as Roche but is a year older, came in as favourite. Though born in Bristol, the vast majority of his fights had been out of America, and of his 33 previous paid starts he had lost only twice, including a defeat against the great Vernon Forrest. His wins included victory over Michael Carruth in Dublin, and a few months after the Roche fight he was to challenge Sugar Shane Mosley for the WBC welterweight title in Las Vegas. At the time he was a world class fighter.

Derek climbed into the ring in Belfast, his kilt-styled shorts now in the purple and gold colours of Wexford. It was a proud moment but one that was to end in despair.

Derek lost in the second round when referee Bill Connors called a halt.

"Looking back, I should have fought a different fight," says Derek. "We had a game plan but it all went out of the window. I'd never known anyone hit like Stone. I saw the punches coming but they still hurt like hell. Usually you see a punch and steel yourself. I did that with Stone and his shots were still like hammers. All credit to him. He's a great fighter.

"Maybe I'd fight him ten times and lose ten times but I'd like to have done better than I did that night. When he caught me the first time I thought to myself 'I'm going to get knocked out here or I'm going to knock you out.' I just thought to myself I'm going to fight him."

Derek caught Stone with two good shots in round one but at the bell he went back to his corner winded after taking a bruising body shot.

In the second round Derek went on the offensive.

I was thinking at the time of what Mark McCreath had said: "Stone's a very dangerous man but we're going to have a technical fight and beat him on technique."

But by now Derek had other ideas.

Stone's American-style bobbing and rolling was evident as he came in low.

Derek threw a left which Stone slipped and Stone replied with a massive right, sending Derek down. He was up on the count of six.

"I was OK when I got up and still ready to have a go. He rushed in and unloaded some more."

Derek rose again determined to carry on. There was then a clash of heads which the referee let go but Derek's nose was bloodied and he was forced against the ropes before the referee stepped in and waved a halt.

"I was disappointed and couldn't understand why the referee was stopping it. My only regret now is that I didn't try and keep out of danger, and left it 'til later to have a go. I've always had the stamina. I feel I'd have had a better chance in the later rounds. But like I say, he could hit hard."

Inevitably, the loss, coming so soon after the Dhami defeat, sparked gossip that Derek might be thinking about hanging up his gloves.

"No. I never thought about it," says Derek.

Talking soon after the contest he insisted there was no question of him quitting.

Co-manager John Celebanski was like-minded. He said: "My one concern is the well-being of my fighters. It's never easy telling a boxer his fighting days are over. I've had to do it before. But this is not the case with Derek. He wants to carry on and the candle hasn't gone out."

The fight though was to mark the end of the Roche-McCreath partnership.

"It wasn't that defeat that did it," insists Derek. "It would have happened anyhow."

Upset by Derek's decision as Mark undoubtedly was, he is not the kind of man who lets matters weigh heavily for too long and was soon back in action with other boxers.

I later saw him in the corner when his man, hard-as-nails cruiserweight Lee Swaby, lost on points to Leeds' Crawford Ashley in Sheffield three or four months later.

Chatting in the lobby afterwards he asked me who I thought had won. I had to say I thought the decision had been right.

"Aw, no man," he laughed. "What fight were you watching?"

And off he went on a verbal analysis for five minutes or so. It was good to see he had lost none of that enthusiasm.

By 2004, Mark was in business, launching the prototype of a hand-held punchball for use in the boxing gyms – a venture that, of course, everyone hoped would do well and bring him deserved success.

Chapter Twenty-Two

The women in Derek's life

I HAD not seen Derek for a little while so rang his mobile number to fix up a chat. There was no reply. The line seemed dead, which I figured might be down to my own less than competent grasp of technology, and so instead I tracked him down to Delaney's Bar. He was sitting, taking a verbal battering from one of the old fellas about a Scottish boxer I had never heard of.

I mention that I have been unable to get him on his phone.

"There's no point trying to ring me on the mobile," says Derek.

"Why's that?"

"Tracei kept ringing me on it," he replies.

That did not seem entirely unreasonable I was thinking, bearing in mind the functions of a telephone.

"She rang me about seven times in a row," sighs Derek. "I was in the car driving along and, well, I don't know, I just chucked the phone out of the window."

I pondered what he said for a moment and pointed out that switching it off might have been an option.

Derek nods as if to say that had not occurred to him.

A week or so after that conversation I call in at Derek's house but he is not in. Tracei answers the door and says Derek is out buying vitamin pills and a few odds and ends.

"Like a new mobile telephone?" I quip, as if I am on a prescription of Oscar Wilde tablets.

Tracei casts me an unnerving look but, thankfully, then smiles.

"He's like a big kid sometimes, you know," she tells me.

My journalistic instinct kicks in and I think this might be an ideal time to quiz Tracei on what it is like to have a professional boxer for a partner.

It is hard to get her to sit still as she busies herself tidying her already spotless home. Tracei's a nice-looking woman, a couple of years younger than Derek, with a down-to-earth attitude typical of Yorkshire females. I get the impression that she has few illusions about men. And I guess that includes me. But she brings me a cup of tea and then sweeps the floor around my feet as I try to chat.

Tracei has been to a lot of Derek's bouts and I ask her if his occupation ever worries her.

She says neither yes or no.

"It's what he loves doing. I know that, so I just let him get on with it."

She pauses a moment and then adds: "I'm always glad when his fights are over. I know he trains hard for them and he takes it seriously. And I also know he's not going to do it for ever."

I ask her what he is like before a fight.

"Quiet," she says. "He's very laid back is Derek, all the time. Very easy going. But when there's a fight coming up he sort of withdraws into himself and doesn't say much. He's one of those who doesn't share his troubles with other people a lot so it's not always easy to know what he's thinking. I just keep out of his way before a fight. Give him a bit of space, you know."

Tracei comes past me with a cloth, wiping down the kitchen units.

Her industry is impressive. As well as working behind a bar, she is also a hairdresser by trade.

"Not much you can do with Derek's hair, though," I say.

She laughs.

I remember Derek telling me how he first shaved his head after one of his televised bouts and he had watched the recording and heard one of the commentators refer to him as 'the balding Irishman.'

"It was straight out with the razor for me after that," Derek had said. "But I liked it shaved off as soon as I'd done it and I've kept it that way ever since."

I chat a little more with Tracei, asking her what she thinks Derek might do once he quits boxing.

"I'd just like him to do something he's happy with," she replies. "That's the only important thing."

And at that point in saunters Derek with young Teighan in tow and the dog padding over Tracei's newly cleaned floor.

"Now then, how's you doing, old mate?" says Derek in his distinct Irish lilt, shaking my hand.

Derek and Tracei have a quick chat about what he has forgotten to pick up at the shops and then he sits down, shaking that shaven head as if to say he cannot be expected to remember everything.

Tracei continues with a spot more cleaning.

One of the things I noticed about their home when I had first visited was the fact that there are surprisingly few mementoes of his boxing career on show. There is a portrait of Derek wearing his Lonsdale belt on the wall but little else and I wonder if that is because Tracei prefers not to have boxing imposing on their home life too much.

"No, not at all," says Derek. "All my trophies, belts and everything are kept safe, I'd not want someone breaking in and pinching the lot now, would I?"

Tracei then feeds a tape of *Bob the Builder* into the video machine for young Teighan to watch before disappearing upstairs to get ready to go out.

"I was asking Tracei what she thought of you being a boxer," I tell Derek.

He shrugs, and then says: "Ah, she's supportive, you know. She comes to most of the fights and that."

"Did she like boxing before she met you?" I wonder.

"I'm not so sure about that, now. I think most women watch boxing if they know the fella who's fighting. Otherwise it seems to me that most of them are not too bothered. Tracei gets a bit nervous before I box but she knows that's what I do and she's never tried to stop me."

"There are some women who box themselves nowadays," I say, expanding the subject a little wider.

"There are, that's true. There's Michelle Sutcliffe in Leeds, I know her."

"So what do you think about women boxing?"

"I don't like it," he replies without hesitation.

"That might be seen as a bit hypocritical," I venture, though I know it is a view shared by a lot of male fighters.

"It might. I've seen some women box and there's a few that aren't all that bad and I'm not saying they shouldn't do it if that's what they want. But if you ask me if I like it then the answer's no. Maybe that's hypocritical or old fashioned, I don't know. But that's how I feel."

He shrugs again and then glances at *Bob the Builder* on the TV screen, indicating, I suspect, that that's the end of the matter.

I change track.

"What does your mother think about you boxing?" I ask.

Derek turns back.

"Like a lot of mothers, I guess she'd rather I was doing something else. She doesn't want to see her boy getting hit. I can understand that, it's normal."

Derek ponders for a moment and then adds with a smile: "She doesn't watch my fights, you know. I remember she came to see me when I won the British title and I'd bought her a ringside seat but she spent the whole of the fight locked away in the toilets.

"She just couldn't watch. I understand. That's what mums are like. She'll sit and watch the tapes afterwards, once she knows that I'm OK."

A little later he whips out his new mobile phone and rings his mother over in Ireland.

"Here, you have a chat," he says passing me the phone.

A charming woman is Liz. She confirms that she cannot bear to watch Derek box.

"I'm very proud of him, though," she adds as if I might doubt the fact. "We all are," she added.

Derek is now smiling. And then he laughs. "I remember the first time my mother came to see me in England after I'd started working at Delaney's. I think she wanted to check the place out – you know, make sure it was a, er, a proper place for me to be working.

"Well, I says to her, you know, 'it's a lovely place, nice and quiet, just a bar for the old fellas to come and have a pint.' My sister who'd come over too, is stood behind her rolling her eyes and saying 'oh yeah.'

"Anyway, I thinks I've got away with this when my mother says: 'Come on I think we'll go and have a look now, shall we.'"

Derek imitates the forced smile he had made to his mother.

They all climbed into a cab and off they set, the mile or so to Delaney's Bar.

"Here we are, then," said Derek on arrival, looking out of the cab window. His face then turned to one of dismay as he saw outside the club his pal Veljko who was working the doors. And squaring up to Veljko, was a notorious local hard man who, as bad luck might have it, had picked that precise moment to visit Delaney's to pick a fight.

Derek knew what was coming and out of the cab he leapt just as his mother began to climb out.

The hard man went for martial arts expert Veljko but was thrown into the air with a single move. Derek guessed the move Veljko would most likely use next to finish the debate and was less than keen for his mother to witness it. He raced up to Veljko and dug him hard in the ribs with a fist. Veljko swung round and saw Derek grimacing at him and then over Derek's shoulder he saw his mum striding over.

Veljko's face burst into a beam and, nudging Derek aside and ignoring the groan from the pavement, he held out his hands.

"Ah such a pleasure to see you, Mrs Derek," he said.

Chapter Twenty-Three

Black and blue in Bethnal Green

DEREK teamed up with seasoned Leeds trainer Terry O'Neill soon after his loss to Adrian Stone.

Terry's association with boxing stretches back more than 50 years. He was an active member of the St Patrick's amateur club in Leeds between 1945 and 1950 before National Service interrupted his career.

In the RAF he qualified as a physical training instructor and on returning to civvy street he put his experience to use back at St Pat's and was fundamental in rebuilding that club.

There were many fine boxers to emerge from St Pat's and Terry's years there were impressive. Apart from his work at the club, he was England manager in 18 international tournaments and in charge of the England Commonwealth squad in 1974 in New Zealand with his lads bringing home a tally of three gold and two bronze medals. In the team were Pat Cowdell, who as a pro went on to win the British and European featherweight titles, and Neville Meade, who became British heavyweight champion in 1981. Terry also managed England at the 1986 Edinburgh Games along with fellow St Pat's stalwart Mick Ryan, who became secretary of the North East Counties Division of the Amateur Boxing Association of England, and was in charge of all the boxing events at the Commonwealth Games staged in Manchester in 2002.

Terry's own career took another path when he turned to train professionals – his ambition being to guide a young Henry Wharton through his career, sharing managership with Leeds-born Mickey Duff.

That was in 1989 and over the next five years Henry won the British and Commonwealth super-middleweight titles before challenging Nigel Benn for the WBC world title at Earls Court in London in February 1994. Henry lost on points over

12 rounds. He went on to fight Chris Eubank and Robin Reid for world titles, by then trained by Gary Atkin, but lost both those challenges, too, on points. Those three losses, though, were the only defeats of Henry's career.

Terry will admit that he still prefers the amateur game to the professional one. And he has seen enough in both camps to hold a respected opinion.

One story I was told concerning Terry involves an incident in America that would be enough to give most people nightmares about the professional game, let alone doubts.

Terry was in the Miami police gym as Wharton prepared for his showdown with Nigel Benn when in walked two men. They looked harmless enough, though they were asking a lot of questions. It being a Friday, it was the day that Terry had his pockets bursting with the folding stuff to pay a long line of Wharton's sparring partners. O'Neill, focused on his fighter, paid little attention to the strangers in the camp until he suddenly felt a heavy prod of a cold gun barrel against his temple and heard loud demands to hand over all his money.

The robbers wrestled him to the ground and with the weapon trained on him he had no alternative but to part with the cash.

"They took the thick end of £2,000," said Terry. "A swift decision was made to get the hell out of there and transfer our training headquarters to Spain."

Derek and Terry kicked off their partnership in less dangerous surroundings than Miami with a six-round points win over Birmingham journeyman Paul Denton in Barnsley.

"That got rid of a bit of the ring rust," said Derek.

It was the start of a double act that was to lead to another world title challenge.

Derek speaks highly of Terry and his training techniques.

"He's very astute, which is both experience and a natural gift. Terry knows I'm a fighter but he knows I can box too and he's tried to bring that side out more. It's often little things he points out – do it this way, what about trying this?"

So you can teach an old dog new tricks?

"Not so much of the old," says Derek. "And they're not new tricks. It's more a case of Terry suggesting it'd be a good idea to do this or to do that for a particular fight and then perfecting it. He's also great at reading a fight, seeing the way it's going and what's the best move next. He can also spot an opponent's weakness, so we work on trying to expose that. There's always a game plan, how we're going to approach a particular fight. It's different from just going into a contest and fighting on instinct and strength. In a lot of ways I wish I'd been with Terry at an earlier age. Teaming up with him has come late in the day but we've not done too bad so far."

I have heard similar comments from other boxers. One fighter told me: "He tells you the right thing in the corner especially when you might be tempted to do summat else and get drawn into summat you don't need.

"He'll tell you what to watch out for, what the dangers are. So you put your trust in him and go out and try to do what he says."

Well, it is nice to know age still counts for a lot. Then again, look at the trainers around the world and see how many of the best are a bit long in the tooth and the value of experience becomes fairly evident.

Derek's next fight under Terry was to be his first venture abroad as a fighter. It was a trip to Holland.

Yorkshire folk, of course, have a lot in common with the Dutch. Naturally, the Dutch speak English better than what we do. They have Rotterdam, we have Rotherham; they have Van Gogh, we have Darren Gough; they have Edam and we have: "eeeeee, that was a nice piece of Wensleydale, Gromitt."

But the idea of the Wexford boy flying the flag for Yorkshire in the Netherlands and coming out on top held a definite appeal for Derek's Tyke fans.

Derek did not disappoint.

The Dutch adventure was on July 7, 2001 in Amsterdam, just a few days before Derek's 29th birthday, though it turned out not to be a Dutchman he fought but a Hungarian by the name of Zoltan Szili.

Szili's record was hardly awesome but he had been in with some quality opposition, including Michael Carruth, Neil Sinclair, French champion Gabriel Mapouka and had himself challenged for the Hungarian light welterweight title.

Derek, though, knew that he needed to impress to merit any further title tilts of his own.

And he did not mess around.

He went to work quickly and Szili was down five times in four rounds before the referee stepped in to save the Hungarian from further punishment.

Hardly surprising that O'Neill was left smiling on the completion of a night's work well done.

"I don't think I've ever seen Derek fight so well," enthused Terry after the encounter. Terry does not usually enthuse for nothing

"He was on top from the first bell to the end and destroyed Szili. I thought the referee should have stepped in much sooner because the fight was only ever going one way.

"It was a great display and Derek was much too strong for Szili. He looked fit and sharp and had trained very hard for the fight. And he's even more determined to hunt another title."

There was to be another fight before Derek's second bid for a world crown. This was against Poland's Adam Zadworny – the man I had interviewed so unsuccessfully after the fight in Barnsley on account of being unable to speak a word of Polish.

Zadworny had been something of an unknown quantity going into the fight, but boasted an unbeaten record.

But Derek was less than impressed.

In spite of a shove early on in the fight that sent Derek to the canvas, Derek soon began to get on top.

His defence seemed to have improved under Terry and he covered up well against the Pole's counter punch.

Having worked out his opponent, Derek started to turn up the pressure, hounding down his man and working hard.

His natural strength began to tell as he hammered the visitor with body blows before a fast combination had Zadworny down for the first time.

A hard right cross finally stopped proceedings.

Back in the changing room Derek was pleased enough with his performance, though hardly ecstatic. More than anything, he seemed irritated by his new pair of boxing boots.

"I was slipping all over the place with them," he complained. "That's why I fell in the first round."

He still had time to pay a tribute to Zadworny.

"He was a stiff puncher, for sure, there's no doubting that."

Zadworny was never quite the same boxer after his encounter with The Rebel. He went on to lose his next half dozen or so bouts. It seems to be a sad fact that for some boxers, a particular contest proves to be a turning point in their career – possibly because they have stepped up a level too far. It is hard to define exactly but it is as if a light goes out and they fail to ever regain the confidence of their winning days.

Another of Yorkshire's top boxers – Bobby Vanzie – was in action that same night in Barnsley, topping the bill in a defence of his British lightweight title.

Bobby is a product of the Karmand amateur club in Bradford, nowadays run by Dave Cariss and his mum Dot. Bobby, or Robert as he is still known at the gym, turned pro in 1995.

His fight in Barnsley was only his second after a defeat that had cost him his Commonwealth title and opponent Anthony Maynard from Birmingham might count himself unlucky to have met Vanzie in a mood to show he was still among Britain's best.

Maynard lasted only 70 seconds.

Vanzie's co-manager at the time, Tommy Gilmour, also, of course, Derek's co-manager, said the ref had been right to stop the fight.

"Maynard was dazed with the first blow to the temple. Bobby stunned him and he wasn't going to recover. His eyes were still glazed when he got back to the corner."

Vanzie had enjoyed a stirring welcome from the crowd as he strolled to the ring. It had been his first fight in Yorkshire for five years.

An amusing footnote to Bobby's fight at the Barnsley Metrodome occurred outside the sports arena. Vanzie's splendid sports car was parked directly outside the main entrance doors.

The car, a brilliant white, had 'Bobby Vanzie British and Commonwealth Lightweight Champion' emblazoned down the side in huge red lettering.

A bunch of fight fans then appeared and, looking at the livery on the car, one of them could hardly disguise his sarcastic glee and said: "I wonder who that belongs to?"

The rest of the lads chuckled, all except one, who remained straight-faced. After a moment's hesitation he announced "I bet it's Bobby Vanzie's."

He beamed widely, clearly delighted at having had the chance to demonstrate uncanny powers of deduction.

Time moves on and I return to this chapter having just witnessed Vanzie suffer a damaging defeat at the hands of a young Russian, Yuri Romanov.

My reason for mentioning it is simply to show how quickly fortunes can change in boxing.

Only a few months earlier, Vanzie had switched camps and signed with Frank Warren, having grown tired of waiting for a European title challenge against Italian Sandro Casamonica.

He then meets a 20-year-old, who has been a professional for a mere nine months, and crumbles.

Vanzie was down four times in eight rounds before referee Mickey Vann called a halt.

Like the warrior he is, though, Vanzie braved the cameras after the fight and paid tribute to Romanov.

He made no excuses but said he felt he had struggled so hard to make lightweight for the fight that it might now be time to consider moving up a division to light-welter.

Once again weight becomes an issue.

Bobby is one of those fighters who can put on a lot of poundage between the weigh-in and the fight.

Some boxers regain between one or two stones stone simply by drinking, says Derek. It is an indication of the dehydration they undergo to make the weight and there is then the question of how their strength has been affected.

Another thought that went through my mind concerning Vanzie's performance was how his unorthodox style had always relied on razor sharp reactions rather than any conventional guard – the ability to dodge shots rather than block or parry. Reactions though fade as a boxer ages and it was a thought that perhaps, at 29, Bobby had lost that edge – because we are talking here of only a split second in timing. Or was it just the weight problem?

Perhaps it was a combination of the two?

Vanzie was caught time and time again by Romanov's right.

There were parallels, with the defeat of Naseem Hamed at the hands of Marco Antonio Barrera when Naz lost on points, unable to stop the Mexican's shots landing. It was a defeat, of course, that cost Naz his world titles.

Derek, who had last spoken to Bobby at a dinner show when they were both guests together alongside Henry Cooper in Leeds, said he could sympathise with Bobby over losing but he provided no further insight.

"It happens," he said. "That's boxing."

Earlier that year Team Roche had clinched a second chance at a tilt for a world title.

It was for a WBU belt – not one of the top world titles but nevertheless a significant prize.

His fight was against tough South African holder Jan Bergman at London's Bethnal Green on January 26, 2002.

No one was under any illusion. It was going to be yet another tough challenge for Derek.

Up to that date Bergman had been stopped twice in his career and on those occasions his conquerors had been the very best of the world's welterweights: Kostya Tzyu and Zab Judah.

But once more Derek was confident.

Terry and his team did their homework and put Derek through his paces in the gym.

My report for the paper after the fight began: *"If courage alone won titles, Yorkshire today would boast a new world champion.*

"Derek Roche fought his heart out at York Hall, Bethnal Green on Saturday night, hauling himself from the canvas no fewer than six times in his bid for the WBU welterweight crown. It was a heroic performance by the Leeds-based Irishman as he tried to battle back from a second round knockdown against class act Jan Bergman.

"The South African showed fast hands and nifty footwork to move well ahead on points by the halfway stage, scoring mostly off long lefts and also opening Roche's left brow by the fourth. But Roche battled on trying to get inside and he took the sixth round. It was a tribute to trainers Terry O'Neill and Mick Tranmer that Roche began making a few inroads.

Even so, his one chance was to land a knock-out blow."

Disaster had struck in round eight when Roche walked on to a right and he was to hit the canvas twice more in that round. By round 10 Derek was again rallying and shared that round. But he was down again in the 11th and again in the twelfth when Bergman unleashed a sweet combination, ending with a short left. Conditioning and guts saw Derek climb to his feet once more to finish the contest and win the appreciative crowd's applause.

The judges' scorecards that night were 117-107, 119-106, 119-106.

It was the third loss in Derek's professional career and his first with O'Neill.

"My big mistake in that fight was I showed Bergman too much respect," says Derek shaking his head.

"It's not that I expected to lose or anything but I should have tried to bully him, intimidate him, given him a hard time. Sometimes you've got to be rough. He didn't mind having a go at me. Like when we touched gloves, he wanted to do it at the beginning of each round and then try and knock my head off while I was off guard. I don't blame him. We're not in there having a holiday. What I'm saying is that I should've been using every trick in the book too instead of being like a gentleman just cos he was Jan Bergman. That was a mistake."

This particular fight came back into my mind more than a year later when Glasgow's Scott Harrison defended his WBO featherweight title against Ireland's Wayne McCullough.

I had seen Harrison win the British title in Sheffield and like everyone else had been more than impressed by his strength and tenacity. But what struck everyone when he boxed McCullough was how big he was compared to the Irishman. He battered McCullough over the 12 rounds but McCullough, never previously stopped in his career, refused to go down.

McCullough's heart was unquestionable but there was controversy after the fight, the argument being that the referee should have stepped in to stop it and save McCullough from unnecessary punishment.

Derek himself has no doubts.

"Yeah, it should've been stopped, that one. McCullough was too brave for his own good."

I pointed out that the same might have been said for him against Bergman.

"No," he says firmly. "That was different. The difference was that right to the end I still had a chance against Bergman. There was always the chance I could unload a big one and knock him out. The difference is that there was no way McCullough was ever going to do that with Harrison. They let it go on simply because it was Wayne McCullough."

He was a victim of his own reputation, then?

"Yes, if you want to put it that way."

As if to emphasise Derek's point, Ricky Hatton, a couple of weeks later, defended his WBU light-welter title against former IBF champion Vince Phillips and Phillips took him all the way, in spite of losing nearly every one of the 12 rounds.

"That's it, you see," says Derek. "Phillips had that big right and even in the last round there was still a chance that he might plug Hatton with it and win."

Chapter Twenty-Four

Town Hall trauma

FOLLOWING the Bergman contest, it was to be another six months before Derek next climbed into the competitive ring.

He had waited a long time for the chance to appear in Leeds.

Most fighters would agree there is something special about boxing in one's home town and Derek was no exception even if Leeds was his adopted home town. It was a fight to relish and one that offered the chance for Derek to regain the British title.

Derek told the press after the fight was announced: "From the first day I started I wanted to fight in Leeds. I class it as my home city now and I just want to do it for everyone."

There was a lot of excitement about the bout. The venue was to be the cavernous Town Hall with the fight televised live on Sky television.

Derek's opponent was Ulsterman Neil Sinclair, defending his crown for the first time.

Sinclair had won the belt stopping Harry Dhami in the fifth round at Glasgow seven months earlier. It had been Dhami, of course, who had taken the title off Derek more than two years earlier. (Dhami was inactive for 12 months after successfully defending the belt twice).

Sinclair's reputation was red hot and no one was under the illusion that this was going to be an easy one for Derek.

If there were any latent sectarian feelings within either camp about the encounter they were laudably not in evidence.

I wrote a preview of the show for the paper, quoting Derek's reaction to the TV pundits: " *'Barry McGuigan has given me no chance and neither has Nicky Piper," said Derek.*

"That doesn't bother me. Being the underdog takes off the pressure," he claimed. "But other people have put a lot of faith in me and I just have to keep my end of the bargain and win.

"And make no mistake I am going to win.' "

I continued the piece in my own words: *"There are many aspects that give credence to Roche's confidence. Home advantage is bound to give him a huge lift. Both men's statistics at first glance look similar. Sinclair, at 5ft 10-and-a-half is the slightly taller of the two men. Roche is 29, Sinclair 28. Roche has had 29 paid starts and Sinclair 26 – both have lost three. Sinclair has 18 stoppages to his credit, Roche 14.*

"But look a little closer and wider contrasts become evident. Roche, for example has fought 166 rounds as a professional compared to Sinclair's more modest 91. Roche's only defeats have been title fights and significantly, many of his opponents have been better quality than Sinclair's.

"Trainer Terry O'Neill said: 'It's fair to say that Sinclair's track record is not as good as Derek's.'

O'Neill's remarks reflect a definite canniness. He is backing his man but at the same time recognises that statistics are often an indulgence of the press and the anoraks.

After all if a fighter has boxed a greater number of rounds, what does it tell us? What is important is what has been learnt during those rounds and significantly how much damage psychologically or physically has been endured along the way.

I continued in this vein, however: *"Sinclair has never gone 12 rounds – in fact his longest fight was when he stopped Paul Dyer in the eighth in Belfast in May 2000. Roche, however, has gone 12 rounds on four occasions.*

"O'Neill said: 'Derek's not suspect on the stamina, he can pace himself.'

I then, once again, added my own observation: *"Bearing in mind both men's reputation as hitters, however, whether or not the fight can go the distance remains to be seen.*

Derek's co-manager Tommy Gilmour had something to add too: *"Tommy Gilmour says: 'Sinclair and Roche is a very exciting prospect and it could be a case of who gets to who first. They can both bang.' "*

Those words of Tommy's were to ring very true – it could be a case of who gets to who first.

The scene was set both in the press and on television and fight night arrived – June 15, 2002.

But what sticks in my mind most is not so much the contest itself but the memory of Derek sitting motionless on a table in the changing room afterwards, his eyes wide open staring straight ahead at nothing.

He looked like a man in shock.

Knowing how much this fight had meant to him, his despair was almost tangible.

I turned to Tracei who was in the changing room. She looked on the verge of tears and we had a brief chat.

A little later I went back to Derek who was shaking his head.

"What's to say?" he muttered looking straight through me. "I didn't see the punch and it put me down. I thought I was OK and I just took my time trying to get my breath back. I could hear the count and was ready to be up on five. I went to stand up and nothing happened. It was like my legs were disconnected from my brain. When they reacted it was too late. I'd been counted out. I just couldn't believe it."

Derek shook his head and repeated the words: "I just couldn't believe it."

In my fight report I fell back on a cliché.

"Boxers are only ever one punch away from glory or defeat."

The report continued: *"Neil Sinclair landed the perfect body shot to end The Rebel's hope of regaining the British welterweight crown.*

"It was all over in round one of their clash at Leeds Town Hall on Saturday night. The title holder from Belfast, making his first defence, unleashed the devastating blow to Roche's midriff and Roche sank to the canvas, failing to beat the count.

"Bitter disappointment then for the popular Wexford man, who had been so eager to impress in his adopted home city.

"But Roche has shown heart and passion in the ring so often that this defeat reflects no shame.

"Roche had yet to find his rhythm or distance in this fight. Throwing a right hook after a left jab, he exposed enough torso for

Sinclair – renowned for his hard punching – to sweep in a clinical blow under Roche's elbow. It was a shot that rendered the body's motor lifeless.

"*As Roche said afterwards, he expected to be up on the count of five but the legs just wouldn't have it.*"

The crowd had been almost as stunned as Derek when he dropped to one knee after the blow for what looked likely to be a straight forward mandatory eight-count. But rising at nine, referee Paul Thomas completed his count with just two minutes, two seconds on the clock.

When I saw Derek again about a week later he still seemed troubled about the nature of his loss.

"It wouldn't have been so bad if it hadn't been in Leeds. But I just feel I let everyone down. I want to say sorry to all the fans."

I was a little surprised that Derek felt he had anything at all to apologise for. Such things happen in boxing. It had not been me and neither had it been anyone else who had taken Sinclair's shot.

Derek even wondered if some people might have thought he had stayed down deliberately.

I tried to dispel him of that notion. The punch had just been one of those that unhooks the battery leads from the brain to the legs.

Derek had shown his heart time and again in previous fights and no one who had seen him box before would ever question his courage.

Trainer Terry O'Neill was philosophical: "It was just one of those punches."

But it remains true that there are some defeats that are particularly hard for fighters to come to terms with.

I read an article by top American boxing-writer Bud Schulberg which exemplifies what it is to lose certain bouts.

He wrote: "*In a lifetime of watching and knowing professional fighters, I've been struck with their kinship with poets rather than tobacco chewing outfielders from Georgia, or teenage wonders at Wimbledon. 'I'm not hurt just embarrassed,' a friend of mine told me after the referee stepped in to save him from further punishment. In the dressing room at the Garden (Madison Square), Archie McBride, a heavyweight I co-managed, stared at the floor after being stopped by Floyd Patterson in seven and mumbled 'I'm okay, I'm okay, I just feel bad you and all your friends had to see me like that.' "*

Schulberg mentions, too, the well-documented case of Floyd Patterson who, having lost his title in a first round KO, donned a disguise complete with false beard and sneaked out of Chicago.

Happily, Derek did not resort to such extremes after his own defeat. He did, though, go home to Ireland for a break.

"It was just a case of being with the family again, people who best understood how I felt," he said.

Chapter Twenty-Five

Fighting back

THIS book now more or less comes around full circle. After the shock of that Sinclair defeat, in what had been his thirtieth pro start, Derek picked himself up once again and proved that his career was not yet over by getting back in the ring and beating Darren Bruce.

That was a victory, a feat, that it would be wrong to underestimate. For many boxers a loss such as that suffered by Derek against Sinclair would have meant their career had reached meltdown point. The psychological damage alone might have ruined many a fighter.

Darren Bruce had been a test – presumably an intentional one – did Derek have the heart to carry on?

Well, he answered that question unequivocally.

As he said: "I loved every minute of it."

He then attended the golden jubilee celebrations of the Leeds ex-Boxers' Association, happy he said to be not yet one of their members.

Time moves on.

Derek has a little more than three weeks before his next contest.

His mind is becoming increasingly focused as the contest draws closer. His work rate is stepped up noticeably.

I call in at the gym and watch him sparring for round after round under the watchful eye of Terry O'Neill's right-hand man, Mick Tranmer. Mick leans on the ropes with stopwatch in hand.

Derek seems to be working particularly on his upper body movement and unloading from angles. By the time the sparring ends, the gym's windows are dripping with condensation and steam billows off Derek's head like clouds from a cooling tower.

He gestures to me with his gloves.

"Fancy a round or two?"

Well, obviously, I would love to. It has been a busy few days on the newspaper and I feel like I am suffering writer's cramp, so a broken nose should round off the week nicely enough.

The busy week has included a rather peculiar story involving the mystery of a missing 1930s painting. The work of art, depicting Leeds lightweight Jimmy Learoyd, has been 'lost' for more than 10 years and the artist's grandaughter is now trying to track it down. As the picture is five foot high and depicts a brilliantined, half-naked man, it is likely that should it be hanging in someone's front parlour it stands to reason it might have been spotted. The chances of anyone coming forward, though, look slimmer than a straw-weight on a bread-and-water diet.

We also ran a story in the newspaper about efforts to save the St Patrick's Amateur Boxing Club. It has been a long saga with St Pat's needing to find a new home, preferably in the same area of Leeds. But the odds seem stacked against them and sadly it looks likely St Patrick's could be consigned to history like several other once illustrious clubs in the district.

Interestingly, while writing up the tale, I came across some old pictures of former world champions Jake La Motta and Floyd Patterson, taken when they were in Leeds as guests of St Pat's, on separate occasions, many years ago. La Motta is smiling, a perfect picture of geniality. He cut a splendid figure when he came to Leeds and proved a popular guest, in contrast, apparently, to how he was perceived back home in America in his earlier years. A well known quote from fellow fighter Rocky Graziano, for example, is: "Me and Jake LaMotta grew up in the same neighbourhood. You wanna know how popular Jake was? When we played hide and seek, nobody ever looked for LaMotta."

Happily, though, experience tells me that the majority of boxers are among the nicest people you could wish to meet. Castleford-born Noel Wilders, is a prime example of a nice bloke who has been climbing the ladder towards the sport's dizzy heights, having just won the European bantamweight title.

The fight was in the French city of Nice. Inevitably, his win prompted the headlines: "Nice one Noel."

But his achievement can hardly be overstated. After just one fight in almost 18 months – that having been on the Roche v Sinclair bill in Leeds – Noel flew out to Nice to box Frenchman Fabien Guillerme in his home city.

Before leaving, Noel had said: "If you're from Cas, you get no favours so I guess I'll just have to go out and do my best."

Noel, a former undefeated British and IBO champion, trained by Mick Marsden in Leeds, lived up to his words and emerged with the European crown.

It is announced that Derek is to fight fellow Irishman Glenn McClarnon, from Carrickfergus, on the televised Huddersfield show. Derek knows he needs to follow up his victory over Darren Bruce with a win against McClarnon if he is to keep alive hopes of another title shot. Looking at McClarnon's record, though, it appears to be yet another tough assignment.

McClarnon has 15 wins against decent opposition in 20 paid starts and, at the age of 28, he is two years Derek's junior.

Meanwhile, another Leeds boxer, flyweight Levi Pattison, announces that he is hanging up his gloves.

The news comes as a bit of a shock. After 16 years in boxing and at the age of 28, Levi was knocking on the door of a British title chance yet has decided not to wait to see if anyone answers.

Manager Michael Marsden's delight at Noel Wilders' European win now turns to disappointment at Levi's announcement.

Levi's explanation is that he had woken up in the morning and simply decided that he had had enough. He said it was like having had a huge weight lifted from his shoulders. Clearly, he feels he is making the right decision and really that is all that matters. His decision to call it a day does nothing to negate his achievements. As an amateur he won the ABA bantamweight title and boxed for England and, before announcing his retirement, was ranked in the British professional top five of his division.

His decision to retire means he will be off the Huddersfield bill on which Derek is due to fight.

My mind is taken off the matter, though, with a phone call from referee Mickey Vann who is due to take charge of the next Audley Harrison fight.

Harrison, not surprisingly, wins but the same night British heavyweight champion Danny Williams is defeated in Germany by Sinan Sam of Turkey.

Both fights were shown on the BBC.

And, as if to prove that boxing is indeed an international passport to sporting adventure, the very next day there is a show in south Bradford. The venue is the Hanover Hotel nestling among industry at the end of the M606.

The hotel had first been used as a boxing venue a few months earlier for another Sunday afternoon show and had proved popular. A lot of Asian fans had turned out to see local boy Nadeem Siddique make his debut.

Siddique, or 'Sid' as he prefers to be called, was fighting again.

Derek says: "There are a lot of Asians coming into boxing now."

Derek smiles and adds: "Even if I wish Harry Dhami hadn't been one of them, it's a good thing. They're bringing with them a lot of new fans. It's good for the sport. Boxing's always appealed to minorities, over here and in America, that's why you get so many Irish, Italian, gypsies, blacks and eastern Europeans. There used to be a lot of Jewish fighters. Now the Asians are taking it up. I guess it helps the communities gain respect; it shows they're prepared to stand up and be counted. It's also a way of bettering yourself plus, let's face it, you don't have to be well-off to start boxing – not like some sports. So good luck to them.

"It's about respect, that's all."

The nature of boxing, of course, demands respect.

The majority of trainers are fiercely loyal towards their boxers whatever their race, colour or creed.

There was one dinner show, for example, when Meanwood trainer Kevin Cuuningham had just arrived at the ring corner with one of the club's Asian lads when a bow-tied diner at a nearby table shouted out to the Meanwood opponent: "Knock the Paki back to his corner shop."

Kevin bristled, his face turned red and turning to the guest, he said: "You'd better button that lip of yours pal or I'll be the one doing the knocking and it'll be you all the way to the fucking hospital."

Back to the Bradford show – the first bout on is Chris Saunders, the man Derek had beaten in his British title eliminator. Saunders beats Richard Swallow of Northampton that afternoon, watched, as it happens, by heavyweight American KO legend Ernie Shavers and rising light-welter star Junior Witter. Many of the fans seem unaware of Shavers' presence, others have to pinch themselves – Shavers is a living legend, reckoned to have been possibly the hardest-hitting heavyweight ever. Opponent James Tillis once spoke of what it was to be knocked out by Shavers: "I was in the land of make-believe," he said. "I heard saxophones, trombones. I saw little blue rats and they were all smoking cigars and drinking whisky."

But that afternoon in Bradford most of the fans had turned out to see local golden boy Sid who was last on the bill.

Being a Brendan Ingle man it was maybe a little ironic that his opponent should be billed as being from the Yemen, home of Naseem Hamed's ancestors. But Sid's opponent turns out to be called Norman (Stormin' Norman, in fact) and is Birmingham based. In his corner is another Norman – better known as Nobby Nobbs. But there is to be no Norman Conquest. Four two-minute rounds later and Siddique, sporting flash, spangled shorts, has won, much to the delight of his many followers.

Nobby Nobbs then packs away his gear, wearing a world-weary expression and heads back to Birmingham, yet another day of boxing behind him.

Chapter Twenty-Six

Gym culture and a stress fracture

DEREK'S fight in Huddersfield is lined up for the same day as a bout in Sheffield involving a talented young Leeds amateur, Levi Powell, from the Meanwood club.

Levi has won the Yorkshire Schoolboys' Championship at 54kg, beating some classy opponents along the way and is about to meet the Tyne, Wear and Tees champion for the North East divisional title.

It has been a privilege to watch his progress over the years. The amateur game has been a source of pride and pleasure for me over the years with my own son Danny, a clubmate of Levi's. It has also provided a lot of smiles.

One incident that still makes me chuckle happened as I drove from Leeds to Sheffield for a Boys' Club contest unaware the Meanwood boxer involved had got a bye. The boxer had rung my mobile earlier to inform me of the fact and to save me a wasted journey. Another lad with me in the car had answered the phone as I was driving and the conversation, I discovered later, had gone along the lines of:

Boxer: "I've got a bye."

Car passenger: "What?"

Boxer: "A bye."

Car passenger: "OK, then, bye."

And on we drove into the night, following the red tail-lights south.

The fact is that boxing, like other sports, provides plenty of laughs and a platform for friendships that can last a lifetime. It is why boxing is more than just a set of contest rules. Camaraderie is one of the main reasons why sport in general is so highly valued by so many. Love for the sport is often passed on from generation to generation. Thus at the Meanwood club we have Kevin, in his seventies, training the lads alongside his grandson Wayne, another coach. And over the years Mean-wood has produced boxers who have themselves set up clubs or become professional trainers – men such as Mark Bateson, his twin Martin, Michael Marsden and Kevin Spratt.

Although boxing is essentially a one-on-one contest, the craic of the gym is one of the sport's big bonuses.

"Forget what you sometimes see on television," says Derek. "That's just to help sell tickets. In the gym, no-one's allowed to get too big for their boots."

I remember one lad, in the changing room after a few rounds of sparring, was reassuring a doubtful coach that he had the stamina to get through a whole bout in his forthcoming fight.

"I don't know the meaning of the word surrender," he boasted.

His pal looked up, a quizzical furrow running across his sweat-soaked forehead, and he muttered: "Aye, but you don't know the meaning of a lot of words."

And there is room for the occasional clown in the boxing gym.

For example there was Roger.

Roger is what you might politely call weighty. He was aged about 11 when he first appeared at the gym and was about 4ft 6in tall. He did not so much tip the scales as bribe them.

Even so he was a regular attender and was gently coaxed along.

Roger, though, was less inclined to punch a bag than ask anyone who would listen if they could guess what he was going to have for tea.

I copped for a lot of these conversations.

"There's a Pot Noodle waiting for me at home," he would say.

"You'll be looking forward to that, then," I'd reply, suggesting he might be well advised to work up an appetite.

He'd push his gloved hand gently against a bag then turn back and ask: "So what's your favourite flavoured Pot Noodle?"

"Er, I don't..."

"Mine's mushroom," he would add, not waiting for a reply. "Have you ever had Pot Rice?"

And so it would go on until one of the trainers chose not to ignore the fact that the only muscles Roger was exercising were his mighty jaw muscles. By setting a standard of fitness no one else could fall below, Roger became a kind of asset.

But by their nature, boxing gyms are intense places with boxers striving hard to reach their physical peak. They are full of people of varying ages and differing degrees of ability.

It takes a special gift to be able to maintain a happy but busy atmosphere. Sometimes it seems that trainers do not recognise their own abilities in this field.

Trainer Kevin, for example, who used to work with Derek's professional coach Terry O'Neill when they were both at St Patrick's, has a keen gift for banter.

Those who miss training are usually treated to a rebuke of one sort or another on their return. One of Kevin's favourites is: "Don't give me no hard luck stories, son, I know 'em all. If it weren't for bad luck I'd have no luck at all."

When Kevin and Harry Pinkney are together in a corner their combined ages come to 150, which must surely be some sort of record? Younger, but just as keen is coach Dennis McCann, only in his sixties, and Dave Powell, a mere youngster in his forties.

I call in at Derek's gym, which is a little more than a mile down the road from Meanwood. There is actually another nearer boxing gym, run by former women's world flyweight champion Michelle Sutcliffe and her husband Gary.

I find Derek skipping hard. With the fight getting nearer the atmosphere seems to be getting tenser.

Hip-hop music beats out loudly from a portable hi-fi by the ringside.

Mick Tranmer is standing by Derek, mopping the floor with regular sweeps. At first I wonder if the roof has sprung a leak and then realise the water constantly dappling the floor is sweat being sprinkled by Derek as he bobs up and down over the swirling leather rope.

I nod to him. He nods back but does not break the rhythm of his skipping. More sweat splashes on to the floor. Mick continues mopping.

It is not a usual sight. There is a notice up on the gym wall informing all boxers they are expected to mop up their own sweat.

It is now only a few days from Derek's fight. I have written a preview of the show for the paper but as often happens the bill has changed by the time the paper goes to print.

James Hare, who is topping the bill, has a new opponent for his defence of his Commonwealth welterweight title. Belfast's Brian Magee is defending his IBO super middleweight belt and young Dale Robinson is contesting the Commonwealth flyweight crown.

Derek's fight against McClarnon is a scheduled eight-threes. I am also keen to see the Robshaw brothers in action. Cousins of former world super-middleweight contender Henry Wharton, the brothers have recently moved back up to Yorkshire after being London based.

Mick Marsden also has a couple of fighters on the bill, Dean Lambert and Danny Wallace, the latter making his professional debut in the UK after moving back to Leeds from America.

February 19 – just three days to go.

I ring Derek at home just to see how he's getting along.

"Not too good," he replies.

Derek explains that he's suffering what he describes as "a poorly foot.

"I don't know what's happened," he adds. "I was in the gym last night, one minute I was fine the next I can feel the foot's a bit sore. I don't know why, I've not knocked it or anything. I didn't do any skipping after that but just went on the exercise bike.

"It's worse this morning. I can hardly stand up on it."

He says that he had spent the whole morning at the hospital.

"They x-rayed it. They don't think there's anything broken but they're not sure because of the swelling. They don't really know what's wrong. It could be a ligament or something."

I sympathise, a bit lost for words as I am all too aware how much this fight means to Derek.

Derek adds: "I can't go to the gym tonight. I'll just go and take a sauna and try to keep the weight down."

Clearly, he is still hoping he may still be able to fight.

"Listen," I say. "it's between you and Terry, but I can't see how you can box if you're not 100 per cent. McClarnon's a tidy fighter, you know that."

"Yeah, I know what you're saying," replies Derek. "You'll have me crying in a minute, mate."

And then he laughs.

"Have you got the foot strapped up, or what?" I ask, suddenly an expert in physiotherapy.

"I've got one of them bandages on to keep the pressure on it."

I witter on for a while longer.

"Hey, shit happens," says Derek.

He then adds solemnly: "It's a big disappointment after all the training that I've been putting in. I'm feeling gutted."

After all this time, I have noticed that Derek still, now and then, lapses into what you might call a "soundbite" – as if he is giving me a quote for a newspaper. It usually follows him having said something that he would probably prefer not to see in print though I reckon it is not as though any newspaper is likely to print a headline that reads: "Shit happens, says Roche."

But then again, being wary of journalists is not such a bad idea. I have only ever been on the other side of the fence the one time, which was when I bought a glass bottle of fizzy water at a supermarket and the bottle exploded at the checkout.

Peering down, I saw my white shirt turning red from the slivers of glass that had punctured my belly. The next day, still squeezing out the splinters, I spoke to a journalist I knew vaguely who had rung me.

I thought we had just been having a chat until I saw the local paper the next day carrying details of my *Superstore Hell*, including quotes from me as if I had just returned from active service saving Private Ryan. A bit embarrassing.

So as Derek likes to say: "Shit happens."

The next day Derek is not at the gym. Trainer Mick Tranmer tells me that he has had to pull out of the fight as was feared because of the foot.

It is a bad blow for everyone concerned.

When I finally catch up with Derek at home, he is wearing a pair of what might be best described as old men's slippers. He shrugs.

He appears less depressed than might have been expected under the circumstances.

"It's frustrating," he admits. "Especially when you think of all that training and watching what I'm eating, especially over Christmas and the New Year."

He shrugs again and says that in the end he has had no option so there is little point in getting too down about it all.

Had it been a championship fight, he said, he might have tried and risked going into the contest but he said that even if the injury was easing he did not think it would stand up to the exertion of a fight.

An added problem, he said, was that his final countdown in reaching the required weight had been spoilt. He had still been a few pounds too heavy with no way of training to lose the excess. He had sat in a steam room to keep the weight low but it had not been enough.

Derek is not over gloomy or at least seems not to be and he adds that one consolation is that if he can fight again in April, all he needs to do, assuming that the foot heals itself, is maintain his present fitness levels.

We chat a while longer before I get up to go, telling him once more that I am sorry about the way things have worked out.

"You'll be even sorrier in a minute," says Derek, holding open his front door. He points over my shoulder.

I turn round and spot a parking ticket stuck to my car windscreen.

Derek's right – shit really does happen.

The weekend arrives. James Hare wins his bout at the Huddersfield show, Dale Robinson wins, the Robshaw brothers win, and down in Sheffield young Levi wins his schoolboys bout.

Derek himself stays away from the Huddersfield show.

"I couldn't face the idea of being there and not boxing," he explains.

Instead he has a pint or two with his dad who is over from Ireland – having already planned his visit before Derek pulled out of the fight.

Two weeks later and Derek's foot is still sore. If anything he says that it feels worse and he can hardly stand on it in the morning. He has been back to hospital where doctors have, he says, injected his foot with dye and scanned it. It is possible he says that he may have a stress fracture that had not shown up on the earlier x-ray because of the swelling.

All he can do is wait for the doctor's report.

Meanwhile there is a special dinner in Leeds to mark the boxing career of Yorkshire-based Tommy Miller whose connection with the sport as a licence holder stretches incredibly back to 1932.

Four of his former boxers are at the dinner, including referee Mickey Vann and Dave Tuohey.

Derek, who had received an invitation, misses the dinner, blaming a mix-up over dates.

As a matter of interest, I ask him how many dinner functions he has attended over the years.

"More than you've had hot dinners," he replies.

He reminds me that he has also been to Elland Road to show his Lonsdale belt to Leeds United fans during the half-time interval and done the same at Headingley for Leeds Rhinos supporters.

He has even ridden on a carnival floats with gala queens.

"I quite like those sort of things, to be honest," says Derek.

Another was performing the opening ceremony at a betting shop in Harehills, bizarrely while wearing boxing gloves.

"Photographers always want you to put the gloves on for their pictures, even if you're signing autographs," adds Derek, his brow knitted as if puzzled by the concept. "There's people out there as must think we do the washing-up in boxing gloves."

I am reminded of the time when Derek's son Teighan was born, just before Derek's encounter with Adrian Stone, and a BBC film crew called at his house. They showed Derek pulling on the boxing gloves at the same time as Tracei was shown pulling on the baby mitts for Teighan.

It was quite touching, I had thought.

Derek grunted.

"I wasn't in the best of moods," he said. "This TV fella comes into my house and starts telling me what to do."

Derek had had to sit in an armchair with baby Teighan on his lap, supposedly reading from a fairytale book: 'Once upon a time, there was a little boy whose daddy was a boxer...'"

Derek, actually the most doting of dads, grunts again.

The medical report comes back, confirming Derek has a stress fracture.

"They say it'll need six weeks before I can train on it again," says Derek who now does sound a little gloomy.

He then adds: "They say it might never mend properly."

Injuries, of course, are the curse for any professional sportsman but they hit boxers particularly hard because out of action means out of pocket. If you do not fight you do not get paid. There are no relevant insurance policies for pro fighters and no clubs offering sick pay.

All Derek can do is wait and hope for the best.

In the meantime his boxing career is in limbo. It is an anxious time for him, his greatest fear being that he may never box again. He prefers, though, to put such thoughts from his head and tries to remain optimistic.

Meanwhile the careers of other boxers continue apace.

Yorkshireman Junior Witter wins a European Union belt at light-welter, beating Belgian champion Jurgen Haeck on the same Manchester bill as Ricky Hatton's successful defence of his WBU crown against American Vince Phillips.

Young amateur Levi Powell goes on to win the English Schools' Championship title.

Castleford's Noel Wilders retains his European title after a technical draw in Reading against Frederic Patrac, his second Frenchman on the trot.

The Huddersfield trinity of James Hare, Dale Robinson and Mark Hobson are now all Commonwealth champions and deservedly attracting plenty of media attention. Interestingly too, across the Pennines young Salford southpaw Jamie Moore wins the British and Commonwealth light-middleweight title, unexpectedly beating Liverpool's Michael Jones in Manchester after coming in as a late replacement for injured Paul Samuels. It is an impressive performance that elevates Moore into the spotlight. Moore's rise has been laudable with only one defeat in 17 outings. Significantly, perhaps, the only man to have beaten Moore was Scott Dixon, the man, of course, whom Derek beat when he won his Lonsdale belt outright.

Almost certainly, Dixon had been at the height of his powers when he lost to Derek and with no disrespect to Moore, the Scotsman was not quite the same man who had KO'd Moore in the fifth round. That, though, was the one blemish on Moore's record.

Chapter Twenty-Seven

An Italian adventure and a move up the weights

DEREK has been waiting for the foot to mend, if not patiently, then at least managing a smile or two.

I ask him if it makes him at all angry to see others he knows doing well while he himself is out of action.

"No," he says. "That's not how I am. I like to see the other lads winning. It's not their fault if I'm out of action. I always cheer on the Yorkshire and the Irish lads."

It is not long after that I see Derek again and he says he feels confident that the foot is strong enough to venture out on a few short runs.

He starts by running on soft grass so as not to put too much strain on the healing bone.

His optimism is returning and he says that he has spoken to manager Tommy Gilmour.

"He says to take my time, but he reckons he'll have a title fight for me soon. Maybe one of these European Union belts and maybe in Italy."

Derek is smiling again.

His glee is obvious, so much so that had he been a footballer he would doubtless have been over the moon.

It is not long before he finds he has been matched – he is scheduled to appear on another bill at Huddersfield and it is not a title bout.

Some observers might be forgiven for thinking that a return to the ring might be a bit sudden but Derek brushes aside any reservations, clearly eager to get his career back on course. It is now seven months since he last fought.

Once more Derek begins to step up his preparations.

Finally, he learns that his opponent is to be Welsh title holder Jason Williams. Williams had won the area title in February in Aberystwyth, outpointing Keith Jones over the 10 rounds.

He had won 15 of his 20 fights to date, with six stoppages to his credit.

What did Derek think of Williams?

"Don't know much about him. Doesn't matter. I'm just planning to get in there and do the business."

Derek's confidence was plain enough. Others were possibly less convinced, myself included. Matters seemed to be moving a mite too fast, considering the fact it was only a few weeks earlier that Derek was hobbling about.

But as usual my doubts proved unfounded and Derek showed there were still miles left on the clock as he disposed of Williams just one minute and 10 seconds into the second round.

Williams was well-built, and 5ft 11in, but his reach advantage was of little effect. Derek put his man on the canvas with two hard rights before the Welshman climbed back to his feet. Williams was down again when Derek unloaded two left hooks and it was then that referee Phil Edwards called a halt.

Derek's foot had thankfully stood up to the test too and he had suffered no other injuries – "just bruised knuckles" he said.

It was the fifteenth stoppage of his career.

The contest had been fought with each boxer weighing-in at just over 150lb.

Soon after, Derek announced that he, Tommy Gilmour and Terry O'Neill had all agreed that Derek's welterweight days were over and all of Derek's future contests would be at light-middle.

"My last two fights have been over the welter limit (147lb – 10st 7lb) and I've felt so much stronger. I feel the power has come back into my punching and I'm better equipped to absorb shots at light-middle."

Derek had been a welterweight since his teens but after all those years the almost inevitable progression of time had finally caught up with him.

"It's just become too hard to get off those last two pounds. When I weighed-in before the Sinclair fight I was two pounds over and had to work it off. I was drained after that and I'm sure that's why I had so little resistance to that shot that put me down. Because I felt weak I wasn't able to recover quickly enough to beat the count."

Thinking back to that night in Leeds the previous summer it was true that Derek had looked drawn. His face looked gaunt rather than lean and had a greyish hue.

In contrast, before the Williams bout he had looked healthy and in great shape.

Pal Danny Thornton, a middleweight, confirmed the difference.

"In the gym when we're sparring I can notice the difference, I can't push Derek off nowadays like I could do. He's got that extra strength to just force himself forward. It makes a big difference."

Derek was back in action again as early as the following month.

This time it was a flight to Italy to appear in Trieste on a bill topped by Liverpool's David Burke, bidding for the vacant European lightweight title against Italy's Stefano Zoff.

Again, it was not to be a title fight, but Derek was still eager to pull on the competitive gloves once more.

It was only the day before leaving Britain that he found out who he was facing. I contacted Matchroom's John Wichussen, already out in Italy, and he said it was 90 per cent certain Derek would box 33-year-old Argentinian Silvio Rochas.

"Never heard of him," admitted Derek.

A week or so earlier Derek had been hoping that he might get to fight Hungarian Mihaly Kotai for the vacant WBF light-middleweight title.

Kotai, however, was matched a few weeks later to fight Russian Akhmed Oligov at the MEN Arena in Manchester.

Unbeaten Kotai is a household name in his homeland and it takes little imagination to realise his management team saw Derek as being too big a threat, especially after Derek's victory over Jason Williams. Understandably, it was prudent to sidestep the Irishman and instead they landed Oligov.

It was an example, though, of a curious characteristic of boxing, that by performing well and impressing, a fighter like Derek can actually harm his short-term prospects by becoming someone to avoid.

It can drive both boxers and fans alike crazy – and anyone who doubts that need only look at the letters column of most editions of *Boxing News*.

Kotai's match with Oligov was broadcast live back to Hungary, which, of course, was a nice earner for the British promoters. But not for Derek. Team Kotai's reluctance to fight Derek might be seen, at least, as being a back-handed compliment, though it was not one that greatly impressed or pleased the Irishman.

Instead, Derek found himself heading for Trieste to meet Rojas. Records revealed that the Argentinian was born in Buenos Aires, went by the inspiring nickname, Mono, had an orthodox stance and was 5ft 7in.

Not a great deal to go on.

To be sure, I found no reference to the fact he looked like the kind of cigarillo-chewing film extra usually gunned down by Clint Eastwood in sixties westerns.

A further examination of his record revealed he had had 83 fights, won 40 and drawn nine.

Most of his contests had been in South or Central America though he had boxed in Europe, including Italy, several times. His most significant opponent had been the legendary Julio Cesar Chavez who had stopped him in the third round in Mexico back in 1993.

Derek's only comment was that he was looking forward to the fight and was eager to keep busy.

It was the culmination of a busy week for the Terry O'Neill camp. On the Monday up-and-coming light-heavyweight Pinky Burton had won in Glasgow; on the Friday, Terry and Mick Tranmer were then in Hull to corner for Danny Thornton as he clinched the Central Area middleweight title against Brendan Ingle-trained Jason Collins and then came Derek's Italian job.

It was stifling hot in Italy. My report of Derek's fight read:
Leeds' Derek Roche flew to Italy with a job to do. It might not have been pretty but he came home mission accomplished.

Italy was an apt venue, with opponent Silvio Rojas looking more like a spaghetti western bandit than a boxer when he climbed into the ring on Saturday night. And there was something of the good, the bad and the ugly about the fight itself.

Good – on a sweltering night in Trieste, Roche, a former British welterweight champion, extended his record to 29 wins, beating a man whose previous opponents had included legendary Julio Cesar Chavez.

Bad – Argentinian Rojas used spoiling tactics and a more than awkward style to survive.

Ugly – Clearly a graduate of the school of dirty tricks, Rojas bit Roche on at least two occasions – once on the arm and once on the chest. He also seemed to try to break Roche's elbow in an arm lock at one stage. Had the contest been more than six rounds, disqualification would have been a near certainty.

Looking bemused after the stifling encounter, Roche said: "I'm glad to win but that fella was a nightmare. He made it the worst fight of my career. That said, it's now time to look ahead to the next one."

The scoring was 58-56, 60-54, and on the referee's card 60-55.

Now with three victories on the trot, Roche stays in the frame for a title shot in the not too distant future.

Arriving back in England, Derek admitted he was less than happy about the contest. The truth was that Rojas had been an impossible fighter to look good against.

One TV pundit joked that if asked whom he wanted to fight next, Derek should reply: 'The man who matched me with Rojas.'

The Argentinian had actually flung Derek to the canvas in round five after trapping his arm and bending it back at the elbow.

"I was in agony," said Derek. "I thought he'd broken my arm, to be honest. Like I said it was just a nightmare."

Derek stopped for a moment and then he added: "Trieste is a lovely place, though."

A short while after returning to Britain, Derek's management confirm that a showdown with Mihaly Kotai is still a possibility after the Hungarian's unanimous decision over 12 rounds against Oligov.

"We are still actively pursuing that fight," says manager Tommy Gilmour.

Derek is pleased by the news, although he has been in the business long enough to know that in boxing nothing is ever certain; deals have to be nailed, stapled, glued and, if possible, welded to the table and even then it might be that at the last minute someone comes in and steals the table.

"That's boxing for you," says Derek – a phrase that could surely serve as a suitable epitaph for every professional fighter.

"All I can do is keep up the training and be ready to fight," he continues. "The rest is out of my hands. But I know Tommy looks after my interests as best he can."

It begins to dawn, however, that the chances of Derek getting a shot at Kotai in the near future are looking slim.

But Derek waits patiently, occasionally speaking on the phone with Tommy Gilmour about other possibilities.

Nothing definite materialises, but Derek remains determined that his next contest needs to be a title fight, or at the very least an eliminator.

"I know I've only a limited number of fights left in me so I want them to be good 'uns," he says, a determined note in his voice.

Meanwhile he carries on at the gym, training and sparring, notably taking his old rival from the amateur days, Lee Murtagh, around the ring in preparation for Lee's looming showdown with Nottingham's Matt Scriven.

The fight is to be a dinner do with Lee topping the three-bout bill vying for Matt's British Masters light-middleweight title.

Once again, Derek is a top table dinner guest along with that Huddersfield trinity of lewading fighters: Hare, Hobson and Robinson who might sound like a partnership of solicitors as opposed to professional fighters but who are undoubtedly popular faces at such shows.

This time the main guest of honour is not directly from the world of boxing but still manages to keep the fans amused.

Thinking back to all the after-dinner speakers I have heard over the years, one that sticks in the mind is former world lightweight champion turned TV pundit Jim Watt .

Watt, appearing in Leeds one evening, introduced himself by recalling his humble beginnings in Glasgow and said that if ever he felt he might nowadays be getting too big for his boots he had only to remind himself that his name was an anagram of "twat."

There was something self-deprecatingly charming about that, I thought.

"Someone pointed it out to me quite recently," he said. "It had nae occurred to me before. Now, I can't help thinking about it all the time."

But back to the Murtagh v Scriven bust-up. And what a bust-up it turned out to be – a street brawl of monumental proportions .

Both men had come to the ring in great shape, an obvious indication as to how much each wanted this one. In the end it was Lee who took the title with Scriven being disqualified in round nine. Both men had already been warned by referee Mickey Vann that the next foul to be committed would be the last. Scriven failed to heed the advice and that, as they say, was that.

It was hard not to feel a little sorry for Scriven, even if Lee had been one round ahead going into the ninth.

It was hard not to feel a little sorry for Mickey Vann either. After taking charge of more than 100 world title fights around the globe he found himself refereeing a war in his own back yard.

And it must have taken some bottle to disqualify Scriven who had brought with him an army of vocal support up from Nottingham.

Anyone who has read Mickey's autobiography *Give*

Me A Ring might recall it was in Nottingham that he once disqualified local favourite Alex Panaski.

Mickey wrote: "The noise was incredible with people booing and calling me every evil name they could think of. And they thought of plenty. Panaski's brother and some of his mates decided I needed a lesson in the finer points of leaning towards the local fighter and came looking for me. Luckily the police found me first and gave me an escort as far as the M1. They parked motorbikes, blue lights flashing, in the middle of the slip-road and told me to put my foot down. I didn't need telling twice."

Credit to Matt Scriven, though, despite his displeasure at the Leeds decision, he was still man enough to congratulate Lee and his corner and even managed to "shake" hands with Mickey at the end, albeit with the hint of a glower on his face.

Disappointment, though, is a part of boxing and there had been disappointments elsewhere.

One of the first had been seeing Yorkshireman Noel Wilders lose his European banatamweight title. Having beaten Fabien Guillerme to hoist the title and then retain the crown against Frederic Patrac, Noel met his third Frenchman on the trot – this time in Sheffield.

Fellow southpaw David Guerault a former undefeated European flyweight champion, demonstrated he was a world class fighter with dazzling hand speed, a devastating left hook and a tight defence. More than anything else, though, he proved he had studied more than a few chapters from the *Boxer's Guide to Dastardly Deeds.* He opened up Noel's face with elbows and forearms as well as his gloves, having taken the initiative after landing a blow on the break, which the Spanish referee chose to ignore.

Noel was stoical about Guerault's tactics, however, saying: "I don't blame him, he came here to do what he had to do and he did it."

Derek says he understands Noel's sentiment all too well.

He said: "Just remember, – it's another world inside that professional ring and you do what you have to do or at least what you can get away with. There's no point complaining afterwards about what goes on. If that other fella in there tries to mix it with you all you can do is try to give some back ... and give it back with interest."

Derek has strong views on most matters concerning his sport and I quizzed him about a series of controversies that had arisen over a short period of time towards the end of 2003. In this country there was a shaking of heads when 34-year-old Jimmy Vincent was denied the British welterweight belt in his match against Manchester's David Barnes.

Barnes went into the fight undefeated in 13 bouts compared with veteran Vincent who was embarking on his 40th paid start with 17 losses against him. Vincent, a traveller, had won a Masters title defeating Ojay Abrahams over a full ten rounds in 2001 and had earned his chance to fight for the British crown after defeating David Walker in an eliminator.

In fact, he had been the only man to beat Walker before Walker challenged for the European light middleweight title against top Russian Roman Karmazin. Vincent's challenge for the British crown, then, was the culmination of a long, hard career and he boxed his heart out against David Barnes winning the fight on just about everyone's card but the referee's.

To the surprise of everyone in the arena, including the TV pundits, the score was announced as 115-114 in Barnes' favour and boos erupted around the arena.

Derek's own view was quite dispassionate. He said that referees could only score a fight as they saw it and in his own experience they tried to be as fair as humanly possible but were not infallible.

"Mind you, you have to remember too, that just because most people disagree with a referee it doesn't necessarily mean that he's wrong. He's in there, nearest to the action, and can see things others can't. Having said that, if you've got three judges then that should be better than having one referee doing the scoring. But sometimes you can wonder about that."

Soon after the Vincent-Barnes fight, and bearing in mind the argument that three judges should be better than one ref, there came a decision in America that took the collective breath away. That followed the Oscar De la Hoya v Shane Mosley fight.

(Maybe there is just something about the light-middleweight and welterweight divisions).

Mosley won on a unanimous decision despite the fact millions of TV viewers and just about everyone in the arena thought the fight had gone the other way.

Derek said it would not be the last major fight to end in controversy but the reality was that in all the hundreds of fights each year, most verdicts were not controversial. He added, however, that everyone – and that included boxers, managers and fans – could be helped by it being made clearer what exactly was required to win a points decision – at the moment, he said, the definition was open to too much interpretation.

"But you have to say that in boxing, judging is, what would you call it? Very subjective. It's not easy to change that. Nothing is ever going to be perfect but I think there is room for some improvements."

I mention to Derek the computer scoring system for amateur championship bouts and internationals. Well, they call it computer scoring but really what it involves is judges pressing buttons simultaneously. In theory it should work well enough but when you watch it on TV and witness the scores flashing up as the contest progresses it is sometimes hard not to wonder if there are some judges who might have been better to let their guide dogs do the marking.

Derek shakes his head.

"I don't see as it works any better than the old system," he says. "The worrying thing is that the system seems to encourage the amateurs to be throwing only the most obvious of scoring shots and ignore other aspects of the game. It means that if you're a tall, lanky boxer you can stay on the back foot and just jab away, picking up the points. If it's the shorter lad who gets inside, the judges all too often just ignore the body shots.

To my mind, the danger is that the amateur and professional codes seem to be growing apart and if it carries on the way it is at the minute, then amateur boxing could become more like fencing than fighting."

Not all controversies are restricted to points decisions, though. A fight, broadcast in the UK, from Los Angeles, was the IBF minimum or straw weight showdown between Colombian Daniel Reyes and Mexican Edgar Cardenas.

Eventually the fight was stopped but Cardenas had taken the kind of punishment that made you want to look away. He had battled on bravely, but with no chance of winning, the referee had failed to step in and the corner had chosen not to throw in the towel.

Derek says: "I'd agree that sometimes a fighter needs to be saved from himself but sometimes on television it's easier to make that decision than it is under pressure at ringside. It's a tough one."

Not so long after – on December 13 2003 – one of the most blindingly poor results ever was recorded when German Sven Ottke was awarded a unanimous decision in his defence of the IBF and WBA super-middleweight titles against England's Robin Reid in Nurnberg.

"That was a bad one," admits Derek. "Every fighter over here, though, knows that if you go over to Germany to fight a German you're going to have to knock your man out. Even so it was a disgrace."

I point out that with the fight having been broadcast by the BBC there must have been a lot of people watching who were probably put off boxing for life.

"You could be right, there. It didn't do boxing a lot of favours," agrees Derek.

He then adds that despite the poor decisions there had been other fights over the same few months that reaffirmed that boxing was still the Noble Art.

Derek mentions Michael Gomez v Alex Arthur in Scotland and then the week after that, over in the States, Floyd Mayweather v Phillip Ndou.

Chapter Twenty-Eight

The arm operation

FOLLOWING his Italian Job, Derek continued to wait patiently for the next assignment. He had hoped September or October might bring news of a contest, but, after an uneventful summer, his elbow was giving him more pain than ever it had.

"That fight with the Argentinian hadn't helped, no way, and the elbow was beginning to feel sore more often," said Derek. "It was still agony for me if I knocked it in sparring or whenever."

Derek went to see a specialist who recommended surgery and a date was fixed.

Almost immediately an offer then came through for Derek to fight young Jamie Moore for the Lancastrian's British and Commonwealth light-middleweight belt.

"It's sod's law, don't you think?," says Derek. "I thought about the offer hard and talked it over with Terry and Mick. My heart told me to take the fight but my head was saying no. I'd only have four weeks to get fight fit and I needed six weeks to prepare for a 12 rounder like that, plus with Moore being a southpaw I knew I'd have to be blocking with my bad elbow. But then again, I'd never turned down a fight before. The main thing, though, was I'd have had to cancel the operation – and I knew I needed it to have it. There was no saying how long I'd have to wait if I was to put the op back. It was a tough one but in the end I decided I couldn't take the fight."

Derek's surgery took place at the NHS hospital in Chapel Allerton, Leeds.

"They had to knock me out for it," said Derek in a manner that suggested the surgeon had used a brick in a sock rather than an anaesthetic.

Derek had seemed remarkably calm before the operation and none the worse for wear the day after.

"It's amazing, look at this, will you?" he said the following day, genuinely impressed by the doctor's skills. All he had to show for the operation were two tiny, cross-shaped incisions either side of the elbow joint.

"I'm already feeling great," he beamed. "They took out three little bones about the size of teeth that had been floating loose inside the joint."

Derek returned to training but the likelihood of a contest before Christmas seemed slim and it looked like being a quiet festive period all round...

On December 26, Leeds and the country as a whole was shocked by the shooting of three police officers in the city.

PC Ian Broadhurst was gunned down and fatally wounded in Dib Lane, Oakwood, a mile or so up from the Harehills district. PC Neil Roper was also wounded in the shooting while PC James Banks was also shot at but escaped unscathed. The officers had been questioning a man they had seen sitting in a BMW outside a betting shop in Dib Lane at 4.00pm on Boxing Day.

Descriptions of the man were circulated on television and in the newspapers and in the ensuing manhunt Derek's pal Veljko was among those arrested. He was taken into custody by armed officers who had burst into his home.

Police, though, were soon chasing another suspect – a Nathan Wayne Coleman, described as an American who had been living in Leeds.

Coleman, it was soon discovered, had worked in the city as a nightclub doorman.

Derek says he had known him but he was not a friend.

"I had met him a few times when he'd been out for a drink. What more can I say?"

And there really is very little more that can be said – for legal reasons – as this book went to print before the prosecution at Newcastle Crown Court. Coleman, 35, had been charged under the name David Bieber at Leeds Crown Court before being remanded in custody ahead of his trial.

Christmas passed and still Derek awaited news of a fight. In the meantime he was granted a professional trainer's licence.

"It was Terry who suggested I ought to get a licence. It gives me another string to the old bow for the future."

To be granted a trainer's licence, Derek, already a licensed fighter, of course, had to appear before a panel of the area council of the boxing board and satisfy them that he was a suitable candidate.

"It meant answering a few questions and showing them I knew what I was talking about," said Derek. "Then I was sent on a medical course for a few days and then I got the licence," he beamed, clearly pleased with himself and knowing that the licence gave him the chance to stay in the fight game after retirement from the ring itself.

Chapter Twenty-Nine

Fighting for the world title at short notice

*'You should have the luck of the Irish, and you'd
wish you was English instead.'*

So wrote John Lennon.

Mind you, he also wrote stuff like: *'I am the walrus, coo coo
g'joob.'*

But whatever your lyrical tastes you could be excused for
thinking the leaves on Derek's lucky shamrock needed a little
more nurturing.

In the spring of 2004, Derek had hoped to be in action on a
sell-out Huddersfield bill but the date came and passed.

And then, on St Patrick's Day, just as trainer Terry O'Neill
packed his bags for a well-earned two-week holiday ahead of
his 75th birthday, and fellow coach Mick Tranmer flew off to
wed in Las Vegas, the call came that Team Kotai was at long
last willing to put the WBF title on the line and fight Derek.

After all this waiting they could hardly have picked a worse
time as far as Derek was concerned.

It gave him less than four weeks to prepare for what was
a world title fight while his trainers were out of the country.
Derek spoke to Terry on the telephone and Terry advised him
against taking the fight at such short notice.

Yet Derek knew it was an offer that might not come again.
He decided to take his chances and immediately got down to
work in the gym.

Leroy Brown, stepped into the breach, to help out Derek
and did a fine job taking him through his paces and building
up his fitness.

Catching up with Derek at the gym I watched him, wrapped
in his boiler suit, work 14 rounds on the pads, sweating harder
than a chilli-munching steel mill worker. I got the job of water
boy, feeding him liquid and dousing his head at the end of

each three-minute period. The shock of the ice-cold water seemed to send Derek's whole body into spasm. He shook his head, swearing beneath his breath and breathing heavily, his face contorted in pain.

This was true torment.

But by the time Terry and Mick were back in Leeds all the hard work looked to have paid dividends. Derek was in great shape, down in weight yet still eating enough to maintain his strength – or so he claimed.

There was no doubt Derek was going into what was to be his third tilt at a world title with a good chance of victory. Sparring with James Hare, followed to help make Derek as sharp as possible.

The fight was set for April 10 at Manchester's MEN Arena, on the undercard of Michael Brodie v Injin Chi – a rerun of their 2003 thriller – a showdown for the vacant WBC featherweight crown.

Being an ever-expanding anorak, I looked up the statistics and studied the form for Derek's fight.

On paper, 27-year-old Kotai was impressive with 27 wins against just one loss. That loss had been the previous September to Zimbabwe's Farai Musyiwa, a man beaten by James Hare in October 2002. Kotai had also been nothing if not prolific – seven fights in 2003, six in 2002 and 12 in 2001 and he had turned pro less than four years earlier. His stoppage rate was good with 13, though many of these had been in his earlier scraps against less-than-impressive opponents – his first nine foes for example could scramble only six wins on their records between them. Even so, there was no doubting Kotai was strong and could bang a bit – Leeds light middleweight Darren Rhodes could confirm that; Rhodes, who was also fighting on the Manchester bill, had gone 10 rounds with Kotai 12 months earlier.

Derek's reaction to all the information was typically cool – "I'll leave it to the other fella to do all the worrying."

It went unspoken, then, that the key concerns for the Roche camp were that Derek was giving away four years to a man possibly at his peak and that Derek himself had not fought for 10 months and had prepared for a championship 12-round battle in less than four weeks.

To expect him to be at his sharpest was asking a lot.

The trip over the Pennines from Leeds to Manchester is only 50 miles and for once the weather on the bleak hilltops was almost sunny.

The fight schedule timetable was dictated by the television contracts – with Kotai v Roche being beamed to Hungary. As a consequence, Derek's fight was the first of the night. It meant that despite a big band of support, the fans were almost lost in the cathedral-like expanse of the indoor Manchester Evening News stadium and some arrived too late to even see the fight.

Derek climbed into the ring adorned in the Wexford colours with his son's name, Teighan, emblazoned on the kilt. He seemed focused on the task ahead. Kotai paced the ring too. He looked as tough as teak.

From the bell Derek announced his intention to get out on to his opponent's toes and harass and bully him as best he could.

It was striking how similar in shape and style Derek and Kotai were – both squat and powerfully built.

As feared, though, Derek's ring rust after 10 months out of the game, if not obvious was evident to anyone who had seen him box before. It was enough to allow Kotai the edge.

By the fifth round Derek was caught by a stray elbow. With blood pouring from an old re-opened wound above the left eye, Derek was in danger of the fight being stopped by the referee. The doctor was called to have a close look. After an inspection at ringside the fight was allowed to continue and come the break, cutsman Benny King got hard to work on Derek's face.

Derek came off the stool at the restart, knowing now that the contest was unlikely to last the distance and he would need a stoppage. He came at Kotai hard. The Hungarian's powerful build and fast hands, though, made him an unlikely candidate for the count.

But Derek kept plugging away – unwilling to give in and determined to see his job through to the bitter end.

By the eleventh round, Derek was trailing well behind. But still he refused to surrender, despite the blood now gushing from the gaping eye wound, blurring his vision. Kotai then caught him after the referee called break and Derek crashed to the deck. But up he got. It was apparent, though, he was still groggy and sure enough he was tagged again by a big left hook and down he went. But, once more, Derek hauled himself up off the deck, stubborn to the end. This time, though, and despite Derek's protests the referee had seen enough and he waved his arms. Derek shook his head, his hope ebbing away like his blood on the canvas. The dream was over. It was the Hungarian's arm that was raised in triumph not the Irishman's; it was the Hungarian who was feted like a lord by the TV presenters who ushered him in front of the cameras to speak of his win to the fans back home.

For Derek there was the despairing trudge out of the spotlight, back to the changing room past the next brace of gladiators waiting in the darkness of the 'theatre's' wings.

Derek sank back on to a bench. No one said much. Terry and Mick began the task of cutting away the bloodied tapes around Derek's wrists and removing his boots. The stitches and analysis would come later.

I looked at Derek and nodded. He smiled – not a bitter smile of despair just a weary smile framed by a bruised and beaten face. His eyes reflected resignation, an acknowledgement, it seemed, that it was all over – perhaps there was a hint of relief – maybe it was dawning on him that he did not have to do this anymore. Or perhaps it was simply exhaustion.

It was only a little later that Derek fell ill and began to vomit.

A doctor was called immediately and Derek was to spend the night in hospital under observation.

It was not until the next day that we spoke again by which time Derek insisted he was feeling fine.

"That's good," I replied. I mentioned what he had looked

like straight after the fight. It was clear he had no recollection I had been there.

His face was blank but then split in a grin as if to say there was nothing to worry about.

He admitted, though, he was unable to remember the final knock down. He also admitted he knew the time to hang up the gloves had come. That, indeed, it was over.

He knew there would be too many six-rounders to get through before any more title shots ever presented themselves if he was to continue as a fighter. It would be too much like starting out all over again, he said. He added that while fighting Kotai there were moves he had wanted to make, punches he had wanted to throw but the body had failed to respond quickly enough.

Hearing him say these words was hard because he was having to admit that an era of his life was at an end. At the same time there was a feeling of relief for those who knew him; it struck me that losing to Kotai had possibly been for the best – to have won would have meant more money, to be sure, but it would also have meant more hard fights against hard men; more chances to have the brain rattled; more risk of paying too high a price for glory.

Derek, doubtless, would have risked all this for another world title shot but the reality was that that chance had passed him by for ever now.

He managed another grin and spoke again of the fight itself.

"I did my best out there. Under the circumstances, I don't think I did too badly. On the night he was the better man and deserved to win it. I gave it my best shot. You can't do no more than that, can you?"

The answer, of course, is you cannot. Win or lose in life you can only ever give it your best shot.

Chapter Thirty

Looking back

AT the very beginning of this book, I wrote that Derek was a fighter whose dedication and courage typified his sport; that in his career he had savoured triumph and suffered heartache.

And hopefully some of the essence of what it is to be a boxer has been revealed in these chapters.

I wonder, though, that knowing what he does now after a decade in the paid ranks and even longer as an amateur, whether Derek would do it all again?

"Bit of a silly question, that," he says.

I point out that, as a journalist, asking silly questions is my job.

"OK, then, I guess the answer is yes," Derek replies. "But that's because I am who I am. There are a few things I'd do different, though."

Like what?

"Well those fights I lost. I look at the tapes, just like I look at the ones of the fights I won. I spot the things which I'd do different."

Anything in particular?

"Well, my first loss was Dhami."

He smiles, then adds with a chuckle: "The first thing I'd have different with that one is not to get my nose smashed to pulp, obviously."

Derek rubs the bristles on his chin in contemplation.

"The thing about that fight, though, is it was one I feel I should have won. So if I was to change anything it'd be that I'd approach it differently. I'd not have gone in there thinking I couldn't lose. I'd have been ready for it.

"As for Stone, I've said before he was a great fighter and losing to him was no dishonour. What I shouldn't have done, though, was just try to slug it out. He could hit harder than any fighter I've been in with. I should've tried to survive and hoped to get the better of him in the later rounds. Also I fought him at the wrong time, I didn't get my head right for it, but that's the way it goes sometimes.

"My big mistake against Bergman was, like I've said before, that I gave him too much respect. It's not that I expected to lose or anything but I should've tried to bully him, intimidate him, given him a harder time. Sometimes you've got to be rough. You've got to be mean."

Well, no one ever said boxing was for softies. But there is an edge to Derek's words that once again hint at a darker side of boxing that perhaps only fighters themselves can truly understand or excuse.

It brings to mind quotes attributed to Pittsburgh's Fritzie Zivic – yet another welterweight.

Zivic who plied his trade for 16 years and boxed 232 contests won a world title in 1941, beating the great Henry Armstrong. Zivic, regarded by many as possibly the dirtiest fighter ever to grace the ring famously remarked: "Kids today think the laces are for tying up the gloves."

(Nowadays, of course, laces are taped, meaning they cannot be used to open up facial wounds).

And Zivic rarely ignored his own advice: "Always work the ref's blind side."

Even he had his limits, though. He once said: "I'd give 'em the head, choke 'em , hit 'em in the balls, but never in my life used my thumb because I wanted no-one to use it on me. But they used to accuse me of that. I used to bang 'em pretty good. You're fighting, you're not playing the piano."

None of this is to say Derek has ever been what might be described as a dirty fighter yet at the same time he has always been one to look after his best interests between the ropes.

"That's a nice way of putting it," smiles Derek. He contemplates what he's going to say next and picks his words carefully.

"I've said to you before: this is the hurt game. There's all sorts of tricks go on inside that ring. Standing on toes, use of the head. Now, using the head, I don't do that deliberately myself but my style means that I do come in low so it's up to the other fella to watch out for himself. But there's lots of tricks. It's like in football, you get shirt pulling don't you? Well they're not supposed to do that but if they can get away with it they do it. In boxing it'll be the other fella's bottom lip you might want to try pulling off and not his shirt – and not just because boxers don't wear shirts. At the end of the day, though, if you're not clever enough to get out of it, you might be best advised to pick another sport."

Derek later moves on to that most painful of defeats – the first round KO – the kind of loss he suffered against Neil Sinclair.

"Yeah, Sinclair," says Derek. "Again he was a good, good fighter. I can't say a lot about it because, let's face it, it didn't last long enough. It was just one of those punches, I didn't see it and wham that was it. But I'd have loved to have got through that knock down – beaten the count – and tried to win in the later rounds. He's not the best of finishers so it might have been a different story. Having said that, he beat me fair and I rate him very highly.

"The other thing about that fight, though, was my weight. I can't complain because it was a welterweight title fight. But I know I weakened myself getting down to 147. After skipping off those final two pounds I was just drained of strength. And I'm sure that's why I couldn't beat the count.

Apart from the losses, I ask Derek if there are other aspects of his career he wished had been different.

"Yeah, but I guess nearly every sportsman can say that. Sporting careers don't last a long time but I don't think I've done too bad.

"I won the British title and that was like a dream come true. And then after that I won the Lonsdale belt outright, and that was fantastic. Then I was thinking about going for the European title or the Commonwealth. Instead I ended up boxing Dhami and after that I'd missed my chance, to go for the others.

"I also wish in a way I'd have been with Terry at an earlier age.

"The irony is that Scott Dixon who I beat defending the British went and took the Commonwealth in his next fight.

"Later on James Hare won the Commonwealth. James is co-managed like me by Tommy Gilmour so when the Commonwealth came up for grabs again the chance went to James not me – he's younger and had more fights left in him, more chance to make money, not just for himself either.

"You've got to remember boxing's a business; it's about money. But I could've made some decent cash defending a Commonwealth. Some of the opponents they pick for the Commonwealth title – well, it looks like easy pickings. Look at some of the fellas James has had. Don't get me wrong. It's not his fault, and no disrespect to him because James is a very good boxer. All he can do is go out and fight whoever they put in front of him. He's got a job to do."

But you would not have minded a few easier opponents yourself?

"I'm not complaining, but most of my fights have been against good fellas. I don't think I've had many easy ones. But the thing is I've enjoyed them all, except Stone but that's because I hadn't got my head right for that one."

Fate or luck often play a big part in a boxer's career too.

I mention to Derek Salford's Jamie Moore, who had surprised everyone when he beat Liverpool's Michael Jones to win the British and Commonwealth light-middleweight title. There is no doubting Moore deserved his victory but his opportunity to fight previously unbeaten Jones came at the last minute after the original challenger Paul Samuels had pulled out.

"Well, that's the way it is, sometimes. All credit to Moore he got the chance and was ready for it, and he was good enough and he took it. You can't fault that."

Derek then returns to the subject of his own career.

"It might sound strange, I've always enjoyed the fights I've had, but it's afterwards you feel it. That's when it hurts. You feel every little bump and lump and every time you touch your head you find a new one.

"At the end of the day you have your ups and downs. But boxing's helped to provide for my family. There's not many in this game, though, make a lot of money.

"One other thing I'd have liked to have done in boxing is fought in America. I'd have loved that. Not just moneywise, but just for the hell of it."

Derek pauses and seems to look a little wistful. He shrugs his shoulders and smiles again.

"Anyway I guess what you should put down is that I've enjoyed my boxing but I don't think I'd be recommending it to anyone else."

It reminds me of something seasoned trainer Vince Flynn, an ex-pro himself, once said to me. "If a lad came up who was a good boxer and good at some other sport like football and he told me he couldn't decide which one to choose, I'd say to him every time: 'Pick football, son.' Boxing's just too hard."

I relate these words to Derek.

"True," he says. "He's right. It's like with my own boy Teighan. If he wanted to box, I wouldn't stop him but I guess I'd rather him pick another sport. Boxing really is just too hard. But it's something that's either in you or it's not and you only really find out when the going gets tough.

"I look back and, like I say, I'm proud at what I've achieved. No one can take that away from me. Not now, not ever. But it's tough. The training's hard, harder than anyone not in the business can imagine. And you've got to dedicate yourself to it if you're going to get anywhere. The worst thing is always having to watch what you eat and drink. And I don't just mean booze, I mean going thirsty when you've been training, just rinsing your mouth out but not swallowing. You come home and you worry about having even a glass of water.

"And there's the pain. You're bruised for days, sometimes weeks after a fight. And what's it all for? You compare what a boxer makes with what your footballers earn and it makes you laugh."

As if on cue, Derek does laugh.

"It's just crazy. But boxing's what I do. It's what I am. Maybe some of us are just born to fight. I'd rather see Teighan playing football, though. We'll just have to see. It'll be his choice in the end."

Derek reflects for a moment and picks up again on the subject of football.

"Pro boxing's different from being a professional footballer or from most other sports.

"If you're a footballer and get injured, you still get paid. In boxing you get injured and can't fight, that's it, you get nothing. You can train hard for months and then end up out of pocket."

It is also not uncommon for a fighter to train for a bout only for the show to be cancelled. The boxer gets no compensation. Exactly that happened to one of Derek's stablemates, cruiserweight Lee Mountford, on three occasions in a row.

"Boxing's a short career, too," adds Derek. "I know football's a short career as well but at least in soccer you can still play the game at a lower level or just for fun if you want. You can't really do that in boxing. You can't go back to being an amateur.

"There's another thing too, while you are boxing you've got to keep winning if you're going to get anywhere. It's not like in football where you might have a bad game but your team still wins. Have a bad day in boxing and that can be the end of your dreams. Have a bad game in football and you might get substituted. But in boxing there's no one going to climb into the ring as a sub and take a walloping for you. You're in there by yourself, just you and your own thoughts.

"Unless you're happy to be a journeyman and are fighting mostly for the pay, you need to keep winning or at least not lose too often. I've never wanted to be a journeyman but I've got plenty of respect for them and what they go through.

"But whatever I've done in life I've always wanted to win. I've always wanted to do my best.

"The thing is, the older you get the harder it gets."

We mention again the Kotai fight.

"Well, he was younger, that's true. But all I would say is that he's a good fighter and on the night he deserved to win. I just wish I'd had more time to prepare. Things might have been different then."

Shortly after the Kotai fight, manager Tommy Gilmour announced in the columns of *Boxing News* that Derek was retiring from the ring.

"Well, he never spoke to me after the fight about it," said Derek, "and he's not been in touch since. As far as I'm concerned I've never said I've quit."

"You told me it was over," I remind him.

Derek glowers.

"But I haven't announced it officially," he says. His voice then mellows. "The thing is now that I'm a trainer it's frustrating because I'm telling fellas to do things I know I can still do myself. I'm helping them to go out and fight fellas I know I could beat myself. It's tough, I tell you."

Derek's dilemma is not uncommon. Good advice from others is that the least painful transition from boxer to trainer or to the ranks of the former fighters is to take a clean break of six months or so from the gym simply to give time for that itch to subside

The number of boxers over the years who must have said to themselves that they will have just one more fight and then quit is beyond calculation.

For many it is the hope of one last good pay-day that is hard to resist.

It is a shame, perhaps, that boxing rarely sees testimonial shows for boxers after a certain number of years in the sport. Such shows might help provide a final purse for retiring fighters. Then again an obvious argument against such a notion would be the temptation it would present for a fighter to hang on and continue past their expiry date simply to qualify for a pay-off. And anyhow, who would organise such events? Boxing is fuelled by profit not charity.

There is a Boxing Board of Control charity, of course,

inaugurated in 1998 that continues the work of the old Benevolent Fund, paying out money to boxers with an immediate financial need. But it is not a pension and is by no means intended to sustain a fighter.

The ex-boxers' associations around the country were launched initially with the intention of helping to provide for former fighters who might have fallen on hard times. But their resources are restricted, particularly nowadays.

In short, most boxers are more or less on their own once their careers are over. It is little wonder that the yearning not to let go is so strong.

Hopefully Derek, deep down, recognises that the time to call it a day has arrived. There had been a reminder not too long before he fought Kotai when his former adversary Adrian Stone announced he was retiring from the ring. Stone, exactly one year older than Derek, made his decision after losing to Argentine southpaw Sergio Martinez in a bid to regain the IBO title at 154lb. The fight had been stopped with 70 seconds of the final round to go.

Bob Mee wrote in *Boxing News*: "It was one of those fights where you instinctively worry for the man on the receiving end and the British Board of Control medical team were quickly into the ring."

Stone was given oxygen and spent the night in hospital as a precaution.

Afterwards he said: "I want to get out while I'm intact. It's time to go."

Derek had nodded at the news.

"Well, there's just the 12 months between us," he had said, referring to the age difference between himself and Stone. "So I guess there's a sign there that the clock is ticking away."

In reality, the Kotai fight was Derek's wake-up call to hang up the gloves. But for many professional sportsmen, and it is not just boxers, life after retirement from their chosen game can seem daunting.

Nevertheless, outside the fight ring, Derek is still a young man.

He has plenty of options, including his intention of staying in the fight game as a trainer. One matter he is adamant about, though, is a wish to quit door work.

"I'm sick of it," he admits.

He also tells me he has had thoughts of a career in some kind of welfare profession in the future, possibly dealing with youngsters. His temperament and intelligence suggests he would be well suited to such work.

Time, as they say, will tell.

But whatever it is that Derek finally does end up pursuing, there is little doubt in the minds of those who know him, that he is, and will always remain, one of one of life's true fighters.

BIBLIOGRAPHY

The One Hundred Greatest Boxers. Mark Collings. Generation Publications.
Facing Ali. Stephen Brunt. Sidgwick and Jackson.
Give Me A Ring. Mickey Vann with Richard Coomber. Mainstream.
The Victorians. A.N. Wilson. Hutchinson.
The Ham Shank. Mary Patterson. University Bradford.
The World Encyclopedia of Boxing. Harry Mullan.Carlton.
Boxing's Greatest Upsets. Thomas Myler. Robson Books Ltd.
Rebellion. Ireland in 1798. Daniel J. Gahan. O,Brien Press.
On The Ropes. Geoffrey Beattie. Indigo.
The British Boxing Board of Control Yearbooks 1990 to 2004. Edited and compiled by Barry J. Hugman. Queen Anne Press.
The A-Z of World Boxing. Bert Blewett. Robson Books.
The Boxing Register. James B. Roberts and Alexander G. Skutt. Robson Books.
Humorous Sports Quotes. Colin Jarman. Guinness Publishing.
Boxing in Leeds and Bradford. Ronnie Wharton. Wharncliffe Books.
Boxing in South Yorkshire. Ronnie Wharton. Wharncliffe Books.
A Fair Fight. Vanessa Toulmin. World's fair Ltd.
The Bare-Knucklers. Dick Johnson. Published by Dick Johnson.